CHILDREN TO A DEGREE

BY HORST CHRISTIAN

Children To A Degree

Loyal To A Degree

Trust To A Degree

Partners To A Degree

Postwar Drifter

Postwar Survivor

CHILDREN TO A DEGREE

Growing Up Under The Third Reich: Book 1

BASED ON A TRUE STORY

Horst Christian

This book is a work of fiction based on a true story.

CHILDREN TO A DEGREE

Copyright © 2013 Horst Christian

www.horstchristian.com

Cover Image Attribution:
Bundesarchiv_Bild_146-1978-016-26
Bundesarchiv_Bild_102-13744

Second Printing 2019
First Printing 2013

ISBN-13: 978-1493734214
ISBN-10: 1493734210

To my classmates and campmates,
who did not survive to tell their own stories about these times.

ACKNOWLEDGMENTS

I would like to thank my readers of "Loyal To A Degree." Without your questions, this book would not have been written.

I would especially like to thank my friends Jerry, Greg and Jon, for encouraging me to write about the mindset of nearly forgotten times.

I also would like to thank my editor, Nicole Etolen, for her excellent work and for allowing me to keep to my timeline.

Christina Haas of ZenthBusinessSolutions.com performed again like a charm. As a matter of fact, she did something like quadruple duty. Starting with formatting the book for Kindle and for the paperback edition, she also designed the book covers and wrote the "blurb," which every author needs. Furthermore, she is now engaged in the publication schedule and the overall promotion strategy of the books in the series.

Chris, I really can't find the words to praise your dedication and guidance sufficiently. Please accept my sincere 'Thank You.'

And then there is Jennifer, my supportive wife, for cheering me on and encouraging me to keep writing and giving me hope that someone might possibly benefit from lessons shared. Thank you, Jenny.

PREFACE

Although this book is based on a true life story, the names of the characters have been changed. However, the people the characters are based on were real, the locations existed, the events actually took place, and the story captures the factual experiences of a young boy growing up under the Third Reich.

FOREWORD

Children To A Degree was originally published as the third book in the series and was written in response to questions I received from readers who had read Loyal To A Degree and Trust To A Degree. They were interested in knowing more about Karl, the main character, and his best friend, Harold, and what their lives were like prior to World War II. Having been born in Germany in 1930 and raised under the influence of the Third Reich, I have firsthand knowledge of how children were raised during that time. However, the questions I received from readers made me realize many people are unaware of how different our lives were from those of children in other countries. Inspired by the questions readers asked, I decided to write Children To A Degree as a prequel to the other books in the series and publish it as Book 1.

All of the characters in Children To A Degree are based on real-life people and so, the book is based on true events. More specifically, the book provides greater detail about the two main characters, Karl and Harold, and their lives as they grew up under the Third Reich and eventually became members of the Hitler Youth. It not only provides a background to their lives in particular, but also paints a picture of how children in general were raised in Germany in the 1930s and 1940s and what was expected of them.

I hope that providing this background about Karl and Harold, readers have a better understanding of how their lives were influenced by the Third Reich and how they came to their own conclusions and ultimately, the reasons behind the choices they made in the other books in the series.

Horst Christian, November 2013

ONE

1940 - Two days after the Easter holidays.

The beginning of a new school year in Berlin, Germany.

Karl Veth was entering for the first time, his new classroom of class Nr. 4 in the Pfalzburger Elementary School. He looked around the room, which featured huge windows that opened to a wide schoolyard and permitted a lot of natural light to enter.

The German elementary school year started with class Nr. 8 every year at Easter and went up to class Nr. 1, which was the 8th school year for the 13 and 14-year old children. (The numbers were opposite from the USA school system. A "first grader" was a student in his last year at an elementary school). Once you were 13 years old, you were not considered to be a child anymore, you were a "young adult", and at the latest, at the age of 14, you had to decide on the trade you wanted to learn in order to earn a living.

However, if the parents decided that their child was smart enough for a higher education, the child could enter a middle school, or high school between the ages of eleven and fourteen.

Karl had entered the German elementary school system at Easter, 1936 before his 6th birthday, which was in July. Due to the wartime shortage of suitable buildings, his previous school was now used to serve as a State Police barrack. The original police barrack was being converted into a military training and command center.

Karl tried to find his friend Harold, who had also been transferred with him and about twenty other children to the school in the Pfalzburger Strasse. It was an all-boy school. There were no integrated classes in Berlin in 1940.

Harold was standing in front of the large double blackboard on the front wall. In their previous school, the blackboard had been very small. The sidewalls of their new classroom were covered with maps of Germany, Poland, and France. He could see that behind the map of France were charts of Holland and of the Scandinavian countries.

In one of the corners was a tall cabinet, which contained teaching aids and material. It also held the feared Rohrstocks (Bamboos or Willow sticks) used to enforce the correct behavior of the students, as well as silence in the 5-minute breaks between the hourly class sessions. Karl wanted to go and greet his friend when the door opened and a male teacher, about 40 years old, entered the classroom.

Instantly the room went quiet. Everybody stood still, hands to their sides, heels together and the big toes about 4-inches apart. Nobody moved as much as an inch; only the eyes of the students followed the teacher, who went to his stand-up desk in front of the room.

"You will address me as Herr Halama."

He opened a folder on his desk and looked at the students. His eyes were gray and hard. There was no smile around his lips, and Karl noted immediately the impeccable suit of the teacher. Not a single wrinkle in the dark blue jacket, and the pants featured a crease, which was as sharp as it possibly could be. He wore a spotless white shirt with a light blue tie.

"First rule. You will not talk unless I ask you. This applies to your 5-minute breaks as well. You are allowed to go to the rest room during the break but never, under any circumstances during the session."

Herr Halama pointed to the boy nearest to him, "You, what is your name?"

"Albert," came the answer.

"Albert what? I want your full name. Don't look down when I talk to you. Look me in the eye. You are not a dog. You are a human being, and I will teach you how to be an adult, so stand straight. What is your full name?"

"Albert Schroeder," the boy answered.

"Alright, Albert Schroeder. Go to the wall cabinet and select a Rohrstock for me."

Albert did not know which one to select, so he took the longest one and handed the stick to Herr Halama.

"This is a pointing stick," Halama announced, "I will use it to point at cities on the maps and to maintain discipline in the class room."

He raised the tip of the stick and whipped it with full force on the top of his stand-up desk. It triggered a sound like a gunshot.

"Second rule. You will rise and stand at attention when I enter the room. You will not sit down until I permit you to sit."

He hit the desk again.

"My folder shows that this is a class of 64 students. I will call out your name and you will answer immediately with 'Present'. Not with 'Here' or 'Ja'. After you answered 'Present' you are allowed to sit. If you don't answer instantly or use any other word than 'Present', you will remain standing during the remainder of session."

Once more the desk reverberated from the hard hit with the stick.

"Gerhard Bruns!" Halama shouted out.

"Present," came a call back.

"Sit!" shouted the teacher.

It was surprising for Karl how fast this teacher established order. Within minutes everyone was seated. Halama scanned the students and continued his first hour of teaching.

"From now on, we will greet each other with 'Heil Hitler'." No more 'Good morning, or 'Good day', and also no more 'Auf Wiedersehen' (Good Bye). These are greetings of the past and for the uninspired, and will not be tolerated. If you want to be a German, then your greeting is 'Heil Hitler'.

"This includes your greetings when you enter a store, or come home. It is possible that your parents did not receive this latest order from our beloved Fuehrer. So I expect you to teach your parents that we are marching into a new time period. If your parents object to the new greeting, I expect you to report them to me and I will report them to the local SS service. They will visit your parents once, to warn them. If a second report occurs ....the SS will teach them proper behavior."

Halama was walking back and forth in front of the class, erect and proud and serious.

"I also expect you to report to me any store owner who does not reply with 'Heil Hitler' to your greeting. As of next week, the Hitler Youth (HJ, boys the ages 14 to 17) will initiate a Streifendienst (control service), which will watch you and the different stores you are visiting. Should they see that you don't use 'Heil Hitler' as your greeting, they will report you to me. Should this happen you will be sorry."

Halama raised his stick again and this time he hit his desk

several times on the sides. He hit it so hard that the wood on the corners splintered. The boys were shocked. Some of them feared that Halama would lose control and hit them instead the desk. They lowered their heads and kept their eyes down.

The teacher almost went furious, "Heads up. Look at me when I am talking. You have nothing to fear if you follow orders. It is when you don't follow orders ……….." He did not finish his sentence. He walked to the first row of students and laid the stick across their desks and lifted the head of the first student forcing him to look at his face, "Now feel the stick and then look at me."

He took his time locking eyes with every one of his students and every one had to feel the Rohrstock.

"Now, let me sum it up, in case one of you is an idiot and did not clearly understand me. You will not talk unless you are spoken to. You will always face me and your greeting will be 'Heil Hitler'. You will report your parents and report merchants and others who don't return your greeting. Or…….." he lifted the stick, "the next time you feel the stick it will be on your behind."

The remainder of the first hour of the new school year was filled with similar instructions. Karl had heard most of them before from his father, who had told him about Herr Hitler's latest orders to the school officials and the Neues Reich (New Empire).

In reality, neither Karl nor Harold knew what all the talk regarding a 1,000-year Neues Reich was about. But they were eager to learn. Upon their 10th birthdays, they would be required (under the Berlin school system) to enter the Jungvolk, (forerunner of the Hitler Youth, which was mandatory at age 14).

Harold was captivated by the discipline, and Karl liked any and all opportunities to increase his knowledge. The only thing he did not like about the 'Jungvolk and the Hitler Youth', was their emphasis on sports. Karl was very small for his age, and it was more than hard for him to run as fast as other boys in his age group. But, he was sure that he would find a way around the test requirements. His grandfather had taught him that whatever he was unable to do with his body, he had the ability to make up with his mind. This was, however, subject to whether he was willing to use it constructively.

Karl was more than willing. He was fascinated by what the mind could achieve and control. His father had taught him to read, write and basic arithmetic at the age of five, and since then he had been obsessed with reading. By the age of ten, he had read Schopenhauer and Kant, Tolstoy, Mark Twain, and Nietzsche. He was ready to tackle the New Age.

This first day in the new school year lasted only 3 hours.

The first hour was filled with disciplinary instructions. The next hour with updates from the battlefields and entering the battle lines on the wall charts. The final hour was learning new songs that glorified Hitler and the Fatherland.

"Boy," said Harold when the boys were dismissed for the day, "Our new teacher got his points across in a hurry. He is also a member of the Nazi party. Did you see the BonBon (Slang for Nazi emblem) on his lapel?"

Karl nodded his head, "Yes, I did. I don't think that he will be our teacher for very long."

"Why do you say that?"

"I don't really know, but his demeanor was that of an officer, and he might be presently in the reserve. My grandfather told me that all the reserve units are being called up to serve. So I think that Herr Halama will pretty soon have to change his nice suit for a uniform."

Harold stopped when they reached the Hohenzollerndam. "We are early. Our mother's don't expect us home before noon. Let's go to the U-Bahn Station (subway station) and see if we can catch a ride to the zoo."

Karl agreed in an instant. Playing in the subway system was their favorite past time, and it was there that they had met for the first time. That was a few months ago in the Zoologischer Garten Station (Zoo station). Karl had entered the subway tunnels through a ventilation shaft and walked underground toward the nearest station platform when he nearly fell over Harold, who had entered the system at a different place. They were almost instantly friends when they exchanged their ideas why they were in the tunnel. They both liked the idea of riding for free all around the city. Both of them would enter the system by using ventilation shafts and emergency exits. They would then walk to the nearest station where they would slip up on the platform and then enter a train, all the time trying to be unnoticed by the stationmaster.

Of course, it was untersagt (not allowed) to walk the tunnels. The third rail, the electrified rail, was a potential danger. But this only added excitement to their game. "How can anybody be so stupid to touch or step on the third rail?" Karl had said when they met.

"Yes," agreed Harold, "When I am home, I don't stick my fingers in a light socket either."

This was the start, but there was more to their friendship. They were essentially loners and had no use for any kind of organized activity. One of the activities they avoided was the singing clubs children in their age group belonged to. Karl could not sing, and neither could Harold. When Harold's parents had changed their apartment, Harold had been transferred to the school Karl attended at that time.

***

One of the class subjects was music. It consisted of singing and learning new songs, which their parents despised because all the lyrics were about marching and fighting. Karl could not understand that he could not start singing when he was ready for it. The idea that he had to wait for the teacher to lift his hand and then wait until the last slow poke in the class paid attention was more than he could stomach.

He liked to do everything fast. So when the teacher announced the title of the next song ....Karl started immediately to hum it. Very loud and out of tune. He hummed the melody because he did not know how to whistle; otherwise he would have.

This unruly behavior expelled him from the music class and entitled him to pick up paper in the schoolyard. When it turned out that Harold also sang out of tune, he was ordered to join Karl in the cleanup detail. This cemented their friendship.

"Are you hungry," Harold asked, pulling a sandwich out of his pocket as they entered the subway system through an emergency exit.

Normally these exits only opened from the inside of the tunnel and led to the rear or the utility basement of an apartment building. They were not marked on the outside, and not locked, but featured a hefty metal handle that had to be moved from below. The boys had overcome this handicap by leaving the handle in the open position. There were not many exits and ventilation shafts they did not know of.

Karl shook his head. His mother had not packed him a sandwich, and when she did, it was only every second day. Food was rationed and scarce. His father, an engineer with precise work habits, had initiated a rationing system of their own. They alternated every other day between two meals or three meals a day. Today it was a three-meal day. Therefore he had not received a sandwich but expected to receive something to eat when he came home.

Harold's father, on the other hand, was a highly placed civil servant in charge of food supply for the Charlottenburg District of Berlin. Karl suspected that this was the reason Harold had a sandwich every day. And, Harold was always offering to share what he had.

"I will have lunch and dinner today, and I had a marmalade sandwich this morning," he told his friend.

They entered the Hohenzollerndam Station, avoided the stationmaster, and took the next train to the Zoo Station. They could have left the station the regular way because there was no check point on the way out, but they walked a few hundred feet underground to an airshaft, which ended inside the zoo property.

Their favorite exhibit was the monkey house, and this is where they went right away. They loved to watch the antics of the spider monkeys, and like always, wanted to stay longer than they had time.

"Let's run," said Karl when he saw that the large clock opposite the zoo entrance almost showed 1:00 pm.

On the way home they saw large paper signs being plastered on the walls in the subway station: 'Careful what you say. The enemy is listening in.'

"What does this mean," asked Harold, "How can the enemy listen to what I say? I don't even see an enemy." He looked questioningly at his friend.

"I don't know," answered Karl, "I will ask my grandfather; he can explain things so I can understand them."

When Karl's mother opened the apartment door, Karl clicked his heels, stretched out his arm as he had seen the HJ boys do, and shouted 'Heil Hitler' at his mother. At first it appeared that he had stunned his mother, but then she laughed.

"Heil Hitler to you too, Karl." She pushed him towards the small bathroom to make sure that he washed his hands. "Is this all you learned today?"

"No," answered Karl, "I learned that I should greet you by saying 'Heil Hitler', and if you don't answer the same way, I am supposed to report you." Karl beamed at his mother, "Mutti, you know that I would never tell on you. But, I will report the sloppy soap man in the store around the corner if he does not answer in the correct new way."

His mother looked at him and shook her head, "You will not report anyone, Karl. You will keep your mouth shut and not give in to the Nazi doctrines. Why don't you like the soap man?"

Karl did not have to think twice, "I think he is a slob. His shoes are always dirty. Even when it does not rain."

Frau Veth silently agreed that her son was right. The man who owned the soap store was indeed a scallywag. But it was news to her that Karl paid attention to such details.

Karl wanted to know, "What is a Nazi doctrine?"

"It is a lot like a guideline, except that Herr Hitler and his charges are forcing these guidelines on us. When you report people who don't abide by these guidelines, you become one of the enforcers. Dad and I are not raising you to become an enforcer of the Nazi regime."

She thought that she had adequately answered Karl's question. Karl thought for a moment.

"Who are Hitler's charges, and what is a Nazi regime?" he asked, "I know what an enforcer is," he added.

Frau Veth handed her son a margarine sandwich, "Here, eat this now. Tonight we have potato soup. I even have a Frankfurter for you. When Dad comes home you can bombard him with your endless questions." She poured him a small glass of milk, "What else did you learn to day?"

Karl thought again for a moment, "Not much. Herr Halama, that is the name of my new teacher told us nothing that I did not knew already. He also does not tolerate any questions. So I was not allowed to ask. So I did not learn anything new."

Frau Veth shook her head, "Karl you learn by listening, and if you listen well, you don't have to ask many questions."

Karl listened to what his mother said but then objected, "I believe that you are correct, Mutti. I only wish that the teachers would explain better what they are talking about. If they would, then I would not have many questions."

TWO

It was not until several weeks later that Karl had a chance to ask his father the questions he had asked his mother.

His father had been working late and also on the weekends due an increased workload. Karl was always sleeping when his father arrived home.

In the meantime, Karl read everything he could get his hands on in regard to the Nazi doctrine. He read Hitler's book 'Mein Kampf' three times, because many of the chapters raised more questions than answers, and he had to resort to other books and newspapers to comprehend what he was reading.

He now knew what a doctrine was about but it still left him confused as to the purpose of the present conditions.

None of the different headlines and terms, which dominated the newspapers, explained in simple words why they had less to eat than a year ago. Their family was not exactly going hungry, but down to two meals a day, every other day, made him wonder what would happen next.

"Papa, you told me that the food is being rationed because of the war. Why do we have a war?"

Herr Veth, 33 years old and prematurely gray, had always invited questions from his son. But this simple question stunned him, because he had no ready answer. "This is a complicated question, Karl. I don't have to work this coming Sunday. We will go to see your grandfather. He will have a better answer than I am able to give you."

Karl was happy to hear that his parents would visit his grandparents. They did so about every other month. His grandfather was a Prussian cavalry officer, and had told him at one time that there was nothing more horrible than a fight of cavalry against cavalry. He was a master in giving simple examples, which Karl could understand.

"Then you don't know why we are having a war?" Karl wanted an answer sooner than next weekend.

"Yes, the simple answer is that our Fuehrer has declared a war, but your grandfather will tell you why."

Herr Veth was uncomfortable with his son's question because it raised an issue he could not understand himself. Hitler's propaganda had claimed that Polish troops had crossed the German border and committed atrocities on German civilians. Herr Veth did not believe a single word of it. Ever since the Olympic Games in 1936, Hitler had openly shown the strengths of the German army. There had been countless parades of drill teams, tanks and modern weapons. All the newsreels of the world had reported about it. Why would a small and badly armed country like Poland provoke a powerful Germany?

"Have you polished my shoes?" he asked his son to divert from the subject.

Karl was surprised by this question. His father owned, besides his Sunday pair, two other pairs of shoes, which he changed daily. Karl could not think of a single morning where he had failed to clean and polish the correct shoes for his father. He was smart enough to realize when he was being sidetracked. It happened a lot lately. Just the other morning he overheard his parents discussing that his mother was pregnant.

"What is pregnant?" he asked, and his mother enquired if he wished a piece of chocolate. While the chocolate was great, and an unusual delicacy, he was not fooled. He went through his father's dictionary and then asked Harold about it.

"Beat's me," said Harold. "I will ask my parents about it. They never sidetrack me."

Karl laughed, "You know why that is, you dummy. You don't ask enough questions."

A day later Harold reported that he had not gotten a direct answer either. "Somehow it has something to do with babies," he said to Karl.

"That's what I gathered from our encyclopedia," answered Karl, "I hope it does not mean that we are getting another child. I already have a three-year-old brother. He is very nice, but small. It will take years until I can talk with him."

***

Sunday came and Karl stood inside the door of his grandfather's apartment. Nobody in the Veth family owned a house. They were a second generation of Berliner apartment dwellers and it was always the father's or the grandfather's apartment, never the grandparents', as this would indicate that the grandmother would be equal to the grandfather. Far from it.

Karl was holding the hand of his little brother Willy, and waited patiently. His parents were allowed to enter the living room, which also served as a dining room, while the grandchildren had to stand at the door until the Grandfather allowed them to enter the room. Sometimes Karl had to wait for several minutes while the adults talked. Today, he did not have to wait so long.

"Karl and Willy, you are allowed to enter and may sit on the two chairs at the table but keep your hands where I can see them." Grandfather Paul was in his typical Prussian Officer mode. Soon after the boys were seated, their grandmother entered the room and handed Willy a coloring book and crayons. The little boy squeaked in delight as he started to thumb through the book.

Grandfather Paul was visibly annoyed. He looked first at Willy and then at Karl's mother, "I told you before that you don't need to visit me until you control your latest child. One more outburst from, what's his name......," he searched his mind, "anyhow, one more unwarranted noise from him and you can take him home."

Karl's mother took Willy on her lap. While she was guiding his little hand with a crayon, she whispered in his ear to be quiet.

"I have a new book for you Karl. You may read it while your father and I talk." His grandfather handed Karl an old and heavy volume of the history of the Mark Brandenburg, which was the county in which Berlin was situated. Karl was happy. He had never seen this book before and a book from his grandfather was a special treat. He hoped that he would be allowed to take it home.

While his father and grandfather discussed the war and the likelihood of air attacks from England, his mother talked quietly to grandma.

"Why doesn't your husband like little Willy?" she asked.

"Oh, never mind him," answered grandmother. "It is not Willy. You should know dad by now. He likes to be in command. I think he is missing his soldiering days. Go in the kitchen and endear yourself to him. Brew him some coffee."

Karl's mother followed the advice and went into the kitchen.

Grandmother sat next to Willy and showed him how to color the pictures. Like always, it turned out to be a very short visit. The grandparents expected and demanded noiseless obedience and the grandchildren were afraid of them.

Parents and their children would visit the grandparents, but never the other way around. Why would they visit grandchildren? They had done their job and raised their own children. Now it was the job of the next generation to raise theirs. Karl had never seen any of his grandparents in his father's apartment.

Before Herr Veth said good-bye to his parents, he turned to his father, "Karl had a question concerning the reason for the war. I hope that you are able to enlighten him."

The former cavalry officer looked at Karl, "Over here, Karl. You never have a single question without a follow-up. What else do you want to know?" He scrutinized his grandson, noticing the polished shoes and the straight upright posture. "I see that you are growing up," he continued. "I will talk to your father about it and maybe I will permit you to visit me more often."

Karl smiled from ear to ear. If he would be allowed to see and ask his grandfather questions maybe twice each month, it could turn out to be a treasure trove of knowledge for him. "I would like to know why we are having a war."

"And?" prompted the grandfather waiting for the second question.

"I would like to understand the terms Nazi regime and pregnant," Karl blurted out.

The white-haired officer looked at his son, who looked away.

"Thunder," said grandpa. "These are loaded questions. But the answer to all three is nearly the same; Die Weichen sind im voraus gestellt." (The switches are set in advance)

He looked at his son, "I guess you have something to tell me."

Herr Veth went to the window and looked out to the courtyard to avoid looking at his father. Discussing with him that the family was expecting a third child was not on his mind.

"Opa, I know what switches are. But I don't understand what you mean," Karl was a touch muddled by what was going on between his father and his grandfather.

"That figures," answered his grandfather. "I will take you for a short trip and show you." He looked at his daughter-in-law, who was also busy studying the wall, "Have your son here tomorrow at 3:00

PM sharp. Not 2:55 PM or 3:05 PM. I expect your courtesy of respecting my time."

Karl was more than happy to spend an afternoon with his Opa, who could see that Karl had another question.

"Yes, Karl?"

"May I bring a friend? His name is Harold and he has the same questions." Karl knew that he was pushing the envelope. His father already shook hands with grandpa and his mother was out the door, holding his little brother's hand.

"Yes, you may, Karl. But only if your friend is well mannered and only if he asks pertinent questions. I am not a baby-sitter for stupid kids."

The next day, Karl's mother delivered both boys at exactly 3:00 PM to her father-in-law. She had a little technique developed to comply with his Prussian punctuality by simply being early and then waiting in front of the apartment door until the time came to ring the bell.

The officer had waited in the hallway to see if she was on time and opened the door as soon as she touched the bell.

"Great," he said. "Nothing personal, but the whole country does not seem to know what time it is. We need to set examples to instill punctuality in the boy."

Karl noted that his grandfather was not shaking hands with his mother, but this was nothing new. He introduced Harold to his Opa.

"I will have the boys back at your place at 5:00 PM" he told his daughter-in-law, then shook hands with Harold. "Karl told me about you. If you have questions save them until I am done. It will save all of us time."

He led the way to the nearest subway station and bought a 'seven station roundtrip ticket' for the three of them. Karl and Harold did not talk to each other. The demeanor of the cavalry officer did not invite any kind of conversation.

They had to change trains at the Zoo Station, then went on to the Gleisdreieck Station, which was the major intersection of trains in Berlin. It was the place where subway trains crossed rails with S-Bahn rails and long-distance trains. S-Bahn stood for Stadtbahn, (city trains).

The S-Bahn operated like the subway on electricity, while steam locomotives powered the long-distance trains.

The sheer maze of intersections of different rails looked like an unsolvable puzzle to the boys. When they arrived at the station, Karl's grandfather led the way across exposed rails to a narrow control building that stood between the tracks. It towered about two stories above the crossings and the top floor featured windows in every direction.

"Anybody home?" he shouted when he opened the door to the stairway.

"Of course, Herr Major," answered a voice from above. "I saw you crossing the tracks, Herr Major. Good to see you again." The voice belonged to a man in the dark blue uniform of a Switch Master. It was obvious to the boys that the men knew each other.

"What brings you here, Herr Major?" the switch master wanted to know.

Karl's grandfather pointed to Karl and then to Harold. "Forget my title, Gustav. This is my grandson Karl and his friend, Harold. They want to know about the function of switches and I could not think of a better place to teach them."

He pushed the boys toward a window in the direction of the main platform of the station. They could see people milling in every direction as they boarded different trains.

"Listen carefully," the Major started to explain. "Berlin is presently a city of four million citizens. People by the hundreds if not by the thousands use public transportation every day. But, there are only a limited number of platforms to accommodate the boarding of the trains. As the trains leave the station, they are routed through switches to the rails that carry them to their destinations.

"This routing is accomplished by Gustav, the switch master; a man with 20 years of practical experience, who is setting the switches. Once the switch is set, the train cannot help itself but follow the rails." The old officer paused for a moment and looked at Karl, "You asked why we are having a war. I answered because the switches had been set in advance. In this case, I mean that the switch leading to the present world war was set by the peace agreement that was dictated to us at the end of the war from 1914 to 1918, which we call now the First World War. The trains, meaning the citizens of this world, are always in motion and the trains will always follow the tracks, which are controlled by the switch masters. Any questions?"

"Yes," answered Karl. "I think I can follow what you said. But tell me, is our Fuehrer, who declared the war, is he the switch master?"

The Major almost puked in disgust. "You have to ask Gustav

here how much knowledge it takes to understand the system. It takes years and years of experience to understand what you are doing when you set a switch. The unsettling problem is however, that anyone, with or without experience, can operate a switch. Go ahead Gustav, show the boys."

Harold and Karl watched as Gustav pointed to a distinct location on the tracks. The boys could discern a switch and Gustav pushed a small toggle switch on the board in front of him. The boys saw that the big rail switch activated and the rails interlocked in a different way than before. Shortly thereafter, a train left the station and followed the track over the switch to another set of rails.

"Wow," said Harold, "I understand what you are saying Herr Major. If I were to start playing with the small toggle switches, I would activate all kinds of large switches down there and if I don't know what I am doing, I would cause all kinds of havoc."

"Excellent," said the Major. "You got it. But I see that Karl is still not satisfied."

Karl shifted his weight from one leg to the other. "I understand that the main switch for the war was set by historical actions. At that time, Hitler was still a private in the army. I also understand, from reading my books that he somehow came to power by feeding the emotions of the people."

"Exactly, your power of comprehension is admirable. What is your question?" The major was proud of his grandson.

"If Herr Hitler is not a switch master with experience, but nevertheless came to the switch board and is now setting all the switches that will cause actions and reactions .... Where is this leading to?"

The major looked at Gustav before he answered, "It will lead first to the answer of your second question. You asked me what the Nazi regime is about. The Nazi regime has been dreamed up by Hitler, who is using and exploiting the Prussian obedience, which is instilled in most Germans, to his advantage and for his purpose. The Nazi regime will lead by necessity to untold misery and eventually to utter chaos. There is no question about it because it is led, controlled and commandeered by a totally incompetent paperhanger. This man is obsessed with ideas of power and control."

"Secondly, the Nazi regime is doomed to failure because it manipulates our people to eventually fight the whole world. The army system is undermined by Hitler's charges, like his storm troopers. His charges killed the leaders of the SA, the very people who helped Hitler to power, by setting fire to the Reichstag."

The white-haired former cavalry officer stroked the few remaining hairs on his head.

"Of course, and true to form, Herr Hitler denied all responsibilities. Matter of fact, he claimed it happened because we don't have sufficient police structures. So, he proceeded by inventing a new one and called it the Secret State Police." (Gestapo)

Again he stopped and reached for Gustav's coffee thermos.

"This police structure is being used to spy on the German people under the pretext of saving the people from enemies within. This is why you see now the slogans all over Berlin, 'Careful what you say. The enemy is listening in.' Herr Hitler wants the people of this country to spy on each other and to report on each other. A simple practice, which right now is being used to eliminate any dissidents."

He took a sip from the hot liquid. "And finally, he installed brutal SS commandos to get rid of experienced officers in our Reichswehr army." The ex-major was not finished but he had to catch his breath once more.

"And now, he replaced our Reichswehr Army with the Wehrmacht, which seems to still be the old guard. But boys, make no mistake about it, the switches are already set and the Wehrmacht will be controlled by the SS, and will eventually give in to them."

"Easy now, Major. You know where this kind of talk will lead you," Gustav interrupted the tirade of the Prussian officer.

"You are right Gustav. But I had to make a point to these boys. They have already been prompted by the Nazi teachers to spy and report on their neighbors and on their parents. What do you expect me to do? Keep my mouth shut?" He was still agitated.

"Please calm down, Opa. Thank you for teaching us something totally different than what Herr Halama is teaching us. But what about the pregnancy term? How does that fit into the switches and all that?"

Gustav smiled when he heard the question. "Let me answer this, Herr Major. The answer is simple. When a couple wants a baby it cannot demand it in an instant to appear here on earth. The couple has to plan for it. In other words, it has to set certain switches in motion for the baby to materialize. The time between setting the switches and the arrival is called the pregnancy term."

"Whoa," said the Major, "this is explaining it rather delicately."

Karl wanted to ask a follow-up question, but his grandfather waved him off, "Not today, Karl. Maybe next time."

Harold had a question of a different nature, "I am not questioning your explanations, Herr Major. But, if this is all true what you have told us, and I believe it is, how come people like our teacher and all the Nazi's around us love the Fuehrer?"

The old cavalry officer looked at Harold, "Smart question, my boy. Our beloved Fuehrer employs the technique of all charlatans who never produce anything. He could not produce a simple salami because he would not know how to make one. So, he does what?"

He looked questionably at Harold, who shrugged his shoulders, unable to think of an answer.

"Come on Harold, it is not a hard question for a boy of your intelligence. Karl? Your turn."

Karl ventured a guess, "He promises something?"

"Correct," said the Major, "When you are unable to deliver, you start promising. Nothing new about it. It has been done for ages. All the religions that promise salvation are a perfect example. You can promise anything you want, if you are not kept accountable to deliver.

"Hitler promises riches, employment, free medical care and prints money without any backing. He promised freedom for the Saarland, the Sudetengau, Austria and Elsass Lothringen, as well as the free city of Danzig. Why? Because he wants their resources as well as their manpower. Once they are under his control, his power grows. Think about it."

He patted Gustav on his shoulders and shook his hand. He said Auf Wiedersehen and not Heil Hitler when they left the control building.

"Thank you, Opa," said Karl when they arrived at home. It was exactly 5:00 PM. Harold also shook hands with the Major and hurried to get home to digest what he had just heard.

"Did you learn anything," asked Frau Veth after Karl settled down with his grandfather's new book in the armchair under the reading lamp.

"More than in the last year in school. I also know now what pregnancy means. I just don't know the exact time frame," Karl was eager to report.

Frau Veth had heard enough and left the room. When her husband came home, she told him, "You have to talk to your father."

THREE

The next few months were filled with air raid drills. For good measure, every week the schools rehearsed a complete school evacuation exercise. There were three different levels of alarm.

The first level was called "L 30". It stood for Luftwarnung 30 (Air warning 30). This meant that the enemy bombers were about 30 minutes away from Berlin. It did not necessarily mean that Berlin was the intended target of the bombers. The enemy planes could bypass Berlin on flight to a different destination. However, it meant that the enemy had penetrated the 30-minute air space of Berlin.

This 30-minute warning served to alert the students who needed 30 minutes to get home. These students were permitted to leave the school grounds to get safely to their families. If the "All Clear" sounded within three remaining school hours, the students were required to return to the school and resume their studies.

The second level was called "L 15", which meant that the enemy was now 15 minutes away. The students who lived 15 minutes away from the school were allowed to leave the schools grounds.

The third level was the full alarm, meaning the enemy was within three minutes away. Bombing was imminent. Everyone had to seek shelter in the basements.

These rules not only applied to the students but to the teachers as well. As soon as Alarm 30 sounded, the teachers in Berlin pushed the students out of the way and ran home.

"You want to make a bet?" Air warning 30 had just sounded the alarm and Harold looked at Karl hoping to entice him.

"What kind of bet?" Karl asked. He and Harold were with the group of the 15-minute children.

"Which one of the teachers will be the first out of the school?" Harold held a pig's lard sandwich in front of Karl. "The winner gets to eat the Stulle." (Berlin slang for sandwich)

Karl was a sucker for pig's lard and Harold knew it. "Not fair to tempt me. I'll take the wager. I bet on Herr Halama."

"That is a sure bet. You have to give me odds." Harold was licking the lard as it dropped off of the gray rye bread. After the lard saturated the bread, it always started to leak. It was now right at the stage where Karl liked it best.

"I also bet that he will not return to the school today, even if we get an all-clear signal within the next ten minutes." Karl agreed to give these odds; he could almost taste the sandwich.

Harold did not even bother to think about it. None of the teachers ever returned to the school, even if the alarm was at 8:30 AM and the all clear came at 9:00 AM.

"That's not a bet Karl and you know it. Here I'll share the Stulle anyway." He let Karl have the first bite, who tried a second attempt at the bet.

"I also wager that none of the teachers will return today." It was just a little after 10:00 AM and it was only a drill, but Herr Halama was already out of sight.

"No bet Karl. It will never happen. I just wonder what school will be like when we have real alarms and air attacks."

He looked at the remainder of his sandwich because Karl had taken an enormous bite out of it. "Here, enjoy the rest. You must be hungrier than I am."

Karl had to admit that all the odds had been in his favor. Neither he nor Harold had ever seen a teacher returning to class.

"I thought the adults are supposed to set examples," remarked Harold.

"I don't know about that," said Karl. "All I can think is that this rule does not apply to teachers."

Harold agreed. The teachers seemed to be the ones who made all the rules while at the same time had none of their own. The boys decided to make their way to the local Jungvolk headquarters. Both of them had turned 10 years old during the summer and as mandated in Berlin, had to enroll in the Nazi youth movement.

The enrollment was during the months of September and February. In 1940, different cities and rural areas in Germany had different requirements. The enrollment was not very complicated. For the most part, a modest form letter from the school sufficed. It listed the personal data from the boys including something like a report card. This report card, however, was very important for both of the boys. Along with their grades, it listed comments from their main teacher regarding their behavior during the breaks.

Both of the boys always studied during recess to get ahead of the class. It was their aim to apply to a Napola school. Napola stood for National Political Educational Institution. It was the top cadet school in Germany. However, they had to wait until they were 11 to apply.

The HJ Scharfuehrer (squad leader) in charge of enrollment into the Jungvolk was about 17 years old. Apparently, his name was Rudy Scholz. It was written in bold black letters on a piece of cardboard slanted against an inkwell.

"Heil Hitler," shouted both boys as they entered his small office at the local police station.

Rudy looked them over before he returned their salute. They looked kind of odd to him because Karl was small and skinny, while Harold was slightly larger than normal.

"Stand three feet away from my desk and stay at attention. Do you know what this means?"

Karl shrugged his shoulders, "No."

Rudy got up from behind his desk, "I will show you." He stood straight and erect in front of the boys, his feet about shoulder width apart and both hands folded behind his back.

"This is the correct way to stand as long as you are in the Jungvolk. You will receive your HJ training when you are thirteen years old."

He sat down again to read the paperwork. "I see that you are studying for the entry exams of the Napola. I assume that you want to excel in sports and physical training. Am I correct?"

Both boys stood as required and looked at each other. Physical exercise was the last thing on their minds. "No," answered Karl. "Look at me. I am small. I could never compete physically with boys of my age group."

Rudy smiled as he studied the boys. "I'll give you that," he said. He looked at his paperwork and then back at the boys. "What about you, Harold? You look like you are strong enough to handle boys in your age bracket."

Harold again looked at Karl, who shrugged his shoulders. "No, I might like physical endurance training, but physical excellence is not on my mind," Harold announced.

Rudy was exasperated by their answers.

"The Napola schools train the leaders of the future. One of their requirements is that you are physically fit." He got up and took a loose leaf binder of a shelf. "Here it is," he started to read. "The applying student has to prove an Aryan lineage dating back at least three generations." He stopped for a moment, "Hmm, I did not know that. I guess this counts me out from the get go." He was black-haired, and his eyes were dark and warm. He continued reading out loud. "The student cannot have any physical impediments like bad hearing or poor eyesight." He stopped again to muster the boys once more before turning back to the manual.

Karl was growing uncomfortable watching Rudy, who now read to himself. He finally could not help himself. He asked quietly, "Is there anything written that I have to be brain dead?"

Rudy interrupted his reading, "What was that?" In his experience, the little boys enrolling into the Jungvolk had always been shy. Normally they were overwhelmed by his office and most of the time in awe of his uniform. This kid in front of him was clearly not impressed. Rudy felt almost challenged. "Come again?"

Karl tried to lock eyes with him as Herr Halama had taught the boys. "I was asking if I had to be a bully to be admitted." He rephrased his question to make sure that the HJ leader was getting the meaning.

Rudy laughed, "No, you don't have to be a bully. Nevertheless, it would help a boy of your dimensions to have some physical training to back up questions like that." Rudy started to like the boy. He had been put in charge of enrollments because of his natural ability to help the boys get comfortable during this process. "Let's shelf the questions regarding the Napola and get back to your enrollment."

He placed the binder back on the shelf and consulted a different one to make sure that he did not miss anything, "First things first. You will meet in this building twice a week in the afternoon. You will be part of a group of about 10 to 12 boys. You will be taught how to stand, how to walk and how to salute. On weekends, your small group will meet with three or four other groups and you will learn how to march in formation." He glanced once more at the boys, "Any questions? If not, I will see you next Tuesday afternoon at 4:00 PM. You are allowed to be fifteen minutes early but not a single minute late. If you are late you will be given a brush and a bucket of water to clean the sidewalk."

Karl raised his hand, "When do we get uniforms?"

Rudy opened a drawer on his desk and handed each of the boys an entitlement form. "Good question. The purchase of the uniform is the obligation of your parents. At this time of the year you are still required to wear a summer uniform consisting of a pair of black short corduroy pants and the regulation brown uniform shirt. Furthermore, you will need to wear dark brown knee socks and sturdy leather shoes."

He smiled and almost laughed when he saw the awkward arm movements of the boys who shouted Heil Hitler as they scrambled out of his office. He knew that it would only take a week or two at the most and the boys would know how to salute.

Neither Karl nor Harold owned a watch but they observed the large clock hanging on the outside of a pharmacy near the police station when they returned on the following Tuesday. There were several other boys of likewise age who looked at the clock to make sure they would be on time. Ten minutes before 4:00 PM they went down the street and entered the police station.

A large sign in the hallway directed them to their assembly room.

Each of the boys shouted Heil Hitler when they entered the room and almost poked their eyes out when they extended their arms in an effort to greet each other. Each one of the salutes was returned by a fourteen year old boy who stood next to a desk. He was dressed in the summer uniform and glanced towards a clock hanging on the sidewall. His manners were relaxed and his voice was distinct but friendly. When the clock showed 4:00 PM, he walked to the door and closed it.

"Alright, line up on the walls around the room. The tallest one over here on my left and then the rest of you line up according to your height. Which means the smallest one will be at the far end."

Karl went right away to the end of the line. Nobody in the room was smaller than he was. Harold, however, stood in front of the line.

"My name is Bernard and you can call me Bernd," the 14 year old announced. Karl, who had an eye for details, noted that the uniform shirt of Bernd must be either new or starched. It looked flat and unwrinkled.

Bernd picked up a piece of paper from the desk and began reading off names. Every one of the boys answered with '*Present*', except for a heavy-built boy who seemed kind of lost.

"Dieter," Bernd addressed the boy, who nodded, "Please make it easy and conform to all of us. We answer the roll call with 'present'.

Understood?" He had an infectious smile. The boys lost their initial uneasiness and instinctively warmed up to him.

"We will spend a lot of time together and we will make a good team. We are called a Jungschaft, which is the smallest unit in the Jungvolk."

Bernd continued, "I am a Jungschaft leader." He pointed to a red and white cord, which extended from his breast pocket to a center button on his shirt, "This little cord shows you my rank. Dieter, come here next to me." He gripped Dieter by his shoulders and turned him so that he stood sideways to the boys.

"Extend your arm straight out in front of you. Fingertips at eye level and fully extended. Now click your heels and shout *Heil Hitler*." Dieter lost his shyness as Bernd turned him right and left to show the boys the proper way to salute. "Now, all together. Raise your arms like Dieter, who will from now on serve as our salute role model."

All the boys lifted their arms as instructed. When it came to clicking their heels it was a little difficult to follow the example. It took a few minutes until Bernd was satisfied.

"You are doing great. Next time we will train on this again until it becomes a part of you. For your next exercise, I will show you how to stand and how to walk. I am not talking about marching, I am talking about walking and standing without slouching."

The next hour and a half passed like a minute. Every one of the boys wanted to please Bernd, who seemed like a brother to them.

"I wished that Herr Halama would be this easygoing," said Harold as the boys left the police station.

"Now, that would be a stretch," agreed Karl. "Herr Halama and easygoing does not even sound right. Something is wrong with that."

They passed a small grocery store that was about to close the doors for the day. The grocery woman carried the vegetable boxes from the outside rack to the inside to lock them up and the grocer was serving his last customers. The sign on the outside showed that the service hours ended at 6:00 PM.

"Let's have some fun," suggested Harold. "We should enter the store and yell *Heil Hitler*, click our heels and then walk out again."

Karl did not think much of the idea, "How can that be fun?"

Harold did not give up, "Come on, Karl, this would be good training for us," he grinned at his friend. "We will walk out without buying anything. Just in and out."

Karl liked the wide grin from Harold but sometimes he thought that his friend had weird ideas, "I don't have any money to buy anything anyway, do you?"

Harold's grin faded faster than the daylight, "No, I never have any money. My mom pays me a few Pfennige (pennies) when I do some household chores, but they always disappear in the piggy bank."

Karl agreed, "Same here. I think when I am grown up I will have a bunch of pennies."

Harold considered the answer, "Me too. You think that we will have enough to buy us some apples?"

"Yes, I guess we could buy some apples but not enough to buy us an orange. My dad says that oranges are very expensive because they come all the way from Spain and we have to pay something like import duty. Did you ever eat an orange?"

"No, never did," Harold answered. "How about you?"

Karl nodded his head, "Yes, once, last Christmas."

The boys had stopped their walk while they were talking and scanned the people in the grocery store. There were no bigger boys around to possibly chase after them.

"Wait," said Harold, "what if the grocer does not return our salute. Do we report him to Herr Halama?"

"No," answered Karl. "My mother said that I am not to report anyone."

Harold was done observing the store customers. "Let's do it. But shout as loud as you can and really click your heels."

He opened the door to the store and the boys stood still for a moment because nobody paid them any attention.

"Heil Hitler!" roared both of the boys together. Their heels clicked like a whip and their arms were extended just as they had been instructed a short while ago.

"Get out!" yelled the grocer. He threw a rotten potato in their direction. The customers grumbled to each other and the boys clicked their heels once more as they turned on their left heel and left the store.

"This was not much fun," said Harold on their way home. "I had hoped for a different reaction."

"What did you expect?" Did you see the grocer's wife? She nearly slipped and fell. Is that what you hoped for?"

Harold shook his head, "I really don't know. But it was not much fun," he repeated once more.

The boys did not know it at the time but two years later, by 1942, the Jungvolk introduced regular store patrols where they did exactly what Karl and Harold had done; except they reported any storeowner who did not answer their salute. Hitler's doctrine worked slowly but it worked. People were afraid to get reported and so it came that everyone shouted Heil Hitler, Nazi's and dissidents alike.

FOUR

During the following year a few things changed in the Veth family. Karl found himself with a baby sister, although he had no clue where she came from. His parents told him something about a big bird, a stork, which apparently had lost its way on a baby delivery route. Luckily for the stork, his mother had been in the right place at the right time to catch the baby and now they had to take care of her.

Yeah, right. As much as Karl trusted his parents he had his doubts. Besides, he had never seen a big bird in the city.

A few days after the arrival of his sister he had conferred with Harold about this issue and the boys decided on a trip to the zoo.

"I don't see any babies," said Harold while the boys stood in front of the Stork exhibit.

"No," agreed Karl. "I don't believe the story anyway. But let's make sure and look up some other big birds."

On the way over to the other birds they ran into a woman wearing a zoo caretaker uniform. "Ask her," suggested Harold, and Karl walked right up to her.

"Excuse me, dear lady, could you please direct us to the baby pond." Karl was polite as usual.

"What baby pond?" she answered seemingly confused.

"The one where the storks get the babies for their delivery route," Harold chimed in to help his friend.

"Oh that one," the women smiled at the boys. "We don't show ponds like that in our zoo. It is out in the country where the big baby lakes are located." Karl smiled back at her and thanked her for the information.

"I don't believe her either. This is a question for my grandpa," he declared to Harold, who suggested that they should drop their investigation for the time being. There were far more pressing issues to attend to.

Lately, both boys used every free minute they had to study for the Cadet school entrance examinations. They even had, for the time being, suspended their excursions in the U-Bahn system. They studied and studied. Their fathers supplied them with school books from the higher classes. By the end of the school year they were so far ahead of their class that they were bored out of their mind during the school hours.

There was nothing the teachers could tell them that they did not already know forward and backwards.

"I am sure that my grades are sufficient," Karl confided to Harold as they carried their report cards home. Report cards were given twice each year, six months apart from each other.

The German report card grading system started with #1 as very good and ended with #6 as insufficient. The only thing better than #1 was a handwritten remark by the teacher such as: excellent, best of the class, extremely advanced and similar comments.

Neither Karl nor Harold had received a number in their last report card. They had nothing but remarks of excellence. But, they also had a remark below the #6 in turnen (physical education).

Harold's remark read: "Unable to catch a ball and unwilling to learn."

Karl's card was not any better: "Objects loudly to ball games by claiming that he cannot learn anything from a ball which is round and only rolls around the ground. He also refuses to run or jump."

"That's about right," said Harold as he studied the teacher's remarks and Karl agreed. Due to shortage of teachers (most of them had been drafted) the class now numbered 128 students. Herr Halama had been drafted as Karl had anticipated and was not heard from anymore. There was even talk among the students that they might get female teachers in the new school year and that the all-boys classes would be integrated with girl students.

"If we get female teachers, I definitely want to be in the Cadet school. I mean my mother is nice and all and she cooks alright but she knows her place when my father speaks." Harold was adamant about that.

Karl loved his mother, but suspected her of being in tune with the Nazi propaganda. His father was quiet when a discussion about Hitler was about to unfold. Karl considered him to be a wise man. But like Harold, he was unable to equate a female with an authority figure.

He agreed with Harold that the best way to learn something worthwhile might be by attending the Napola. But, he had heard from his father that the Napola too demanded a certain amount of physical education.

In addition to that, his father could not fully prove their Aryan linage. Due to the destruction of some records during World War One, some of the birth records from their great-grandparents had been lost. These were two strikes against him.

Harold on the other hand could prove his Aryan ancestry far beyond the requirements. He was also physically strong and might overcome the remarks on his report card.

The examination for the Napola took six days. In the German test system there was no provision for multiple choice answers. All the answers had to be in writing, about a minimum length of 70 words. If the answer was less than 70 words but was correct, you still lost points for failing to give sufficient examples. If the answer was over 100 words and correct, you lost points because you 'rattled' on.

In short, your answer had to be precise and to the point.

Both boys passed the academic requirements with flying colors. A week later their parents received the final results. Harold had been accepted to a school specializing in sciences. There were over 30 Napola schools in Germany at that time teaching political leadership, sciences and linguistics. Karl had been rejected. No reason was given. Karl's mother was even more disappointed than Karl.

"How could this be?" she asked her husband, who was also disappointed. "Karl is just as smart as his friend Harold." Herr Veth did not answer. He thought that he had let Karl down in his research of their Aryan lineage.

Karl was thinking already in a totally different direction. "Among other things, you have taught me to roll with the punches. And roll I will. I will make you proud of me. Just give me some time," he announced to his parents.

"What do you intend to do?" asked his worried mother.

"I have an idea," answered Karl, "but before I tell you I need to gather some additional information." He turned to face his father. "I would like to talk with the school director. Could you please go with me?"

Herr Veth was surprised. In his school days the students avoided the principal like the plague. Yet his son wanted a meeting. "Of course I will go with you," he answered Karl.

The next day, Karl went to the school office and obtained all the propaganda leaflets flaunting the benefits of a KLV (Kinderlandvershickung) camp, or children evacuation camp. The school authorities wanted to entice the parents to send their children out of the city, preferably to relatives in the country. If the parents did not have any connections in the country, the schools offered evacuation camps. The children would be housed on farms or, sometimes, in resorts.

The benefits were obvious. The students would be safe from the bombing attacks and could study without air raid interruptions.

An additional benefit for the parents was the fact that in the near future all of the unimpaired fathers would be drafted and the mothers might also be drafted to work in defense plants. Since the evacuation camps were provided without any costs to the parents they were an ideal solution.

Karl's next move was an unscheduled visit to see Rudy at the Jungvolk office. "Heil Hitler," he shouted as he entered the room.

He clicked his heels and was careful to stand at attention until his salute was returned. Rudy remembered the boy. Not by name, but he had seen him twice a week attending the afternoon gatherings.

"What was your name?" he asked as he scrutinized the boy.

"Karl Veth," came the answer.

Rudy liked what he saw. He noticed the polished shoes and the correct position of the summer regulation cap on the head: two fingers wide above the right ear, three fingers wide above the left ear and four fingers wide above the eyebrows. Many of the boys could never get it right. But Karl wore his cap as if he were a role model. His belt buckle was shiny and the belt was spotless.

"Rudy," began Karl, "I applied for the Napola but got rejected. However, I know that I passed the academic requirements and here are my report cards to prove it." Karl handed Rudy his report cards and stepped back to resume his position of standing at attention. "I would like to join a KLV camp, but not with boys in my age group. I'd like to join as a study assistant for the younger children. Is there any way that you can give me an assignment as a Jungvolk reporter?"

Rudy looked at the report cards and was amazed when he read all the remarks. "Explain, Karl, and stand at ease."

Karl moved his left foot forward and shifted his weight to his right leg. "Well, I could write about the camp activities for our Jungvolk paper. But that is not all. My father and I have a meeting with our school principal coming up. It would be helpful if I could receive a letter from your office attesting to my discipline."

Rudy understood. "You want help from the Jungvolk to obtain a position in a KLV camp."

Karl beamed in anticipation. "Yes, Rudy, can you do it?"

Rudy liked the idea. "Why not? You could write for the Jungvolk periodical as well as for the school paper. Besides that, you could serve as a role model for the 8 to 10-year-olds. I will take it up with our Bann leader," he said. The Bann leader was the adult and highest ranking leader in the Jungvolk. "If he agrees with your idea, you will receive more than a letter of recommendation. You will receive an assignment the school will be unable to ignore."

Karl saluted and then had another question: "How old are you now, Rudy. I mean, will you have to join the army and will I see you again when I come back from camp?"

Rudy was not sure of his answer. "I am close to seventeen and I could volunteer to join the Navy. But, I am sure that we will see each other again. Come back in a few days and pick up your assignment." Karl liked the last part of the answer. He was encouraged that his plan might work. His next job was to convince his parents of his idea.

But first he wanted to consult with Harold. He wanted to see him anyway to say goodbye.

"Tell me, Harold, what you think of my plan?" he asked his friend after he had explained to him what he had in mind.

"I think that it is a great idea. Why did you not tell me about it earlier?" Harold answered.

"I did not think about it earlier because I expected to join you in the Cadet school. I am sorry that I did not make it." Karl was really sorry when he said it, but Harold grinned back at him.

"One other benefit," Harold said. "If you get into a KLV camp you might avoid a female teacher." Both boys had been scared of that possibility.

"How would you approach your parents if you were in my shoes?" Karl asked.

Harold thought a moment. "Isn't it clear? Your mother has her hands full with your sister and your brother. If you leave for camp it would not be any different than if you would have left for a Napola. I would just ask them for advice as to the location of the camp. I think you have a choice, or?" Harold was not sure about that.

"I think that I do but all I really know is that the camp is always for a six-month duration," Karl answered.

"Yeah, six months is also my first term away from home," Harold scratched his head.

"In a way I am almost sorry that we have to part. We have not really begun to explore all of the subway system." Harold looked expectantly at Karl as if he wanted to take a fast excursion. Karl agreed.

"We will do that when we are together again. You might not like the school and I might not like the camp. We could be back faster than we think." The boys shook hands. Harold had to report for a three-day introduction course starting the next day in Potsdam and Karl went home to explain his grand idea to his parents.

"Well this is great!" his mother exclaimed when he was done. "You will make a great contribution when you tell the children about Herr Hitler."

"Mutti, I am not telling them anything about Herr Hitler. I don't know much about him and grandpa says that he is an incompetent quack."

"But you said that you would be on assignment from the HJ," (Hitler Youth) his mother objected.

"Mutti, I am only in the Junkvolk. The HJ starts when I am 14 years old. And, my assignment will not include talking about the Nazis." Karl was happy that his mother was in favor of him leaving for camp. But he did not share her enthusiasm for Hitler.

"Well, then you have everything under control, Karl, and you don't need me to see the principal," his father concluded when he came home and Karl's mother told him about Karl's plot.

"Yes, I think that I do need you when I go and see the principal. I need you to show him my report cards and tell him that you are supporting me," Karl implored his father.

"No Karl, this is your idea. I trust you enough to do this without me. So, you go alone. Stand up straight because you can be proud of your report cards. They are your accomplishments and not mine. Assert yourself when you get questioned. However, if the principal questions my support he can send me a note. Then, and only then, I will go and talk to him."

Herr Veth was sure that he was doing the right thing. However, Karl's mother was of a different opinion.

"You should go with Karl. He might not be able to express himself in front of the principal."

"No, my dear," Herr Veth said, shaking his head. "This is not how this works. Karl conceived this plan, so he knows best how to get it across or defend it when needed. We are raising adults, Vera. We don't do Karl any favor by doing the work for him and keeping him on a child level." End of discussion. The master of the house had spoken.

***

A few days later Karl went again to see Rudy.

"Here is your assignment." Rudy handed Karl a sealed envelope.

"Is your father going with you to see the principal?" he asked.

"No," answered Karl. "My father supports me but I need to do this by myself."

Rudy looked at the boy in front of him. "Karl, wake up. There is nothing left for you to do. You succeeded already. You are holding in your hand an assignment which is directly from the Bann leader. Your school is obligated and, if necessary, forced to honor it. Your dream, or whatever you wish to call it, is coming true. Congratulations."

Karl did not know what to think. A few days ago he had an incomplete thought and now he was holding an assignment in his hand.

"Does it always work so fast, Rudy?" he asked.

The squad leader came around his desk and locked eyes with Karl.

"What went fast?"

"This here. My dream from conception to reality."

"There is something you don't get, Karl. Nothing went fast. How long did you study to obtain your grades?"

"Over a year," answered Karl.

"How many class breaks did you sacrifice for your studies?"

"All of them. It was not a big deal, I like to study."

"How often do you shine your shoes?" Rudy drilled.

"Well, before I go to bed, of course. And at noon too."

"Let me explain something to you, Karl, because there is a lesson in it. Whenever you pursue something, you might not get what you want or aim at, but you will always obtain results. If you don't like the results, you can benefit from your efforts by adjusting your aim."

Rudy shook a stunned Karl by the shoulders.

"You earned this assignment, Karl, by studying for the Napola and then by adjusting to the results. Get it? Nobody handed you this assignment out of the goodness of their heart. You earned it."

Rudy let go of Karl and returned to his seat behind the desk.

"What do I need to do now?" Karl asked, still dazed from Rudy's lecture.

"Nothing special," said Rudy. "Hand the letter to your teacher and wait for departure instructions. By the way, where do you wish to go? You have a choice of the Baltic Sea or the BavAryan mountains."

"The Baltic Sea would be nice," answered Karl and then continued, "but don't I have to ask the principal for an assignment to a lower age group?"

"No, Karl. I liked your idea when you explained it to me. It made sense. We, the Bann leader and the leadership of the Jungvolk, already took care of the details."

Karl almost forgot to salute when he went out the door.

"This is amazing," cried his mother when he came home and showed her the sealed envelope. His father said nothing, but Karl could see that he was pleased.

FIVE

Karl received his travel orders two weeks later. In the meantime, he tried to get some questions answered by his grandfather. The demeanor of the Prussian cavalry officer had changed during the past few months.

Karl did not know exactly why or how, but his opa was now a lot friendlier to his mother. He did not order her around anymore and during some visits he even tolerated giggling and other noises from his brother and little sister.

When his grandfather had heard about Karl's decision to join a KLV camp, he told his son that he wished that his grandson would visit him at least one more time before he left.

"I am glad that you showed up without your Hitler uniform," he announced to Karl when he opened the door for the family to enter. "I'll be ready in a moment. We will go for a walk and maybe to the garden. It is easier to converse without any interruptions." Karl gathered that the grandfather meant the interruptions from his brother and sister.

A few minutes later they were walking down the Pariser Strasse and turned into the Emser Strasse. Karl's grandfather maintained a small garden lot in this area. He leased it from the city of Berlin and grew potatoes and strawberries and a few bushes of gooseberries.

Karl told his grandfather how he had obtained his assignment and about the lesson he had received from Rudy. "I wonder if you have something to add?" he asked.

The old officer took his time before he answered. "Your Rudy has it about right. I would have put it a little differently. If you take certain actions and don't like the results, you should change the actions which produced the unsatisfactory results. However, in your particular case he was right."

He opened the main gate leading to the individual garden lots.

The walkway dropped a few feet below the street level.

"You failed in your original attempt to gain admission to the Nazi school." Karl could hear the contempt in his grandfather's voice. He was sure that it was directed to the school and not to him.

"But then you used the result of your actions, your report cards and your general accomplishments, to assist you in reaching a different goal." He turned and they entered a small side trail leading to a shaded bench and sat down. "Others might call this self-serving, though in your case I call it very smart. Well done, Karl. I am proud of you." Karl turned red in embarrassment. His grandpa had never called him smart before.

He tried a question he had never dared to ask but had been bothered about for a long time.

"Opa," he began, "why don't you like my mom?"

The old man bent down to pick up a twig and played with it while he answered.

"Karl, I like your mom. I actually like her a whole lot. She is a good woman and a good mother. I just don't like her fixation with the Nazi movement."

Karl thought for a moment before he asked, "What do you mean by that, Opa?"

This time the answer came faster. "I mean that your mother has her head in the sand. Meaning she does not want to see or hear what is really going on in Germany. Even if she thinks or maybe believes that there is some underlying historical reason for the war, she is totally blind to the fact that the Nazi's persecute dissidents and that we are printing money without any backing."

Karl had to think again. "Sorry, Opa, I don't understand."

"It's easy, Karl. When a government prints money it creates a currency. If this currency is not backed by a gold reserve or receivables, such as a national product, then this money will become worthless in trading with other countries. Eventually it will self-destruct." He broke the twig and picked up another one.

"To make it even simpler, Hitler is printing money to meet the payrolls of the military and to pay for Germany's armament. People in this country accept it, but the world will not stand by and accept it as something of value."

He looked around to find another twig. Karl could see that his grandfather was nervous.

"And, that my mom does not see it or understand it...this is what bothers you, Opa?"

"No," the old man shook his head. "Your mother is no dummy. She understands and is able to see it, alright. It bothers me that she refuses to see it. It's no use, Karl. It is the timeless question if believing is a curse or a blessing."

"This went over my head, Opa."

"I know," answered the old soldier. "It goes over the head of many people. But I will keep it simple for you." He had found a smaller twig and played with it again, twirling it around his fingers.

"When a man is lost in a desert and walks west because he believes there is water and then finds it, his belief was a blessing because walking in any other direction would have led to his demise. However, if he walks west but the water is in the east, then his belief is a curse because he will perish."

"The man in this example is unable to help himself because he does not know where the water is. However, if your mother would open her eyes she would know. Instead she chooses to stick her head in the sand. And, this is what bothers me, Karl."

"Thank you, Opa, I think I understand." Karl looked up to his grandfather, happy to hear that his mom was not a dummy. He already knew that she was in favor of the Nazis.

"Opa," he started again, "I will be something like a helper, I guess, for the younger children in the camp. Is there something you can teach me or tell me I should know?" He was eager to make the most of the time with his grandfather.

"When do you leave, Karl?"

"In seven days, Opa. Do we have to go home already?"

"Yes, Karl, I promised your grandma to bring you back within an hour. Do you know that she baked a cake in your honor? It is supposed to be a surprise for you."

Karl was indeed surprised. His Oma baked wonderful cakes but only for birthdays and Christmas. He was all for going back in a hurry.

"I don't like surprises," said his grandpa as they went up the stairs to his apartment. "I like to keep my eyes open and always know what is going on."

Karl was astonished to see that his grandma had not one but two cakes waiting for him. The coffee party lasted over two hours and his grandpa even conversed with his mother. This had never happened before. Maybe Grandpa mellowed out. He did not understand what that meant, but he had heard his father mentioning it.

***

There had been some British air raid attacks during the last few months. They had been directed at some of the railroad stations but missed most of the time. They did, however, wipe out a few apartment buildings.

His grandfather had taken the time to show him the damage and informed him that this was only the beginning of what he called *extensive destruction* which was sure to follow. Karl had noticed that since these bombing attacks, the school authorities had sent letters to the parents to enroll their children in the KLV camps.

Karl had told his grandpa about this and the old man had told him the same thing: *This is just the beginning, soon it will be mandatory.*

Now, as Karl was looking out the rear window of his grandfather's apartment, he pondered about everything the old officer had told him. He had gone to the window to give the impression to his parents that he was not listening to their discussions but he was already taking the advice from his opa to keep his eyes open. In this case he kept his ears open; he wanted to know what was going on.

What he heard was not of great interest to him because the conversation was about funeral expenses in the case of fatalities from an air attack. The family consensus seemed to be that the Nazi party should pay for all of it while his grandpa maintained that this was a moot issue. *"The bombs will take care of it. There will be no one left to bury."* Karl figured that this was strictly a subject for adults but somehow he did enjoy hearing his mother talk in the presence of his grandpa. Even his grandma had something to say. Could it be that the air attacks somehow got the family closer to each other?

"Enjoy," said his grandma when she handed him a packet of leftover cake. Karl was in 7th heaven as he went down the stairs. One hand held his little brother and the other the cake. He could manage this anytime.

While there were some dimmed lights illuminating the staircases, the streets were totally blacked out. The few automobiles they passed on their way home had hoods over the headlights. A tiny slit in the hood emitted a tiny bit of light. Karl wondered how the drivers could see anything in this darkness.

He, along with his brother and parents, had large illumination buttons on their clothing. The button had some kind of phosphor coating and you had to expose it to a lamp before you were going out. The light from the lamp 'loaded' the button and for a little while-maybe five minutes-the button emitted a soft glow. Not enough to illuminate anything. That was not its purpose. The button was glowing to be seen by others passing by and to prevent people from running into each other. It worked pretty well for a short while but by the time the Veth family had reached their apartment dwelling, the buttons had lost their power.

"Karl, keep holding hands with your brother. If he falls we will have a hard time finding him," his mother instructed him almost every minute while she was carrying his little sister. His father walked besides his mother, holding her arm, and when the sidewalk narrowed he inquired: "Karl, are you still behind us?"

It was not often that the Veth family walked at night but when they did, it was nothing short of an adventure.

At home all the windows were covered with black out curtains and Karl was instructed to walk from room to room to inspect the windows, making sure that no light could be seen from the outside.

Aside from these self-imposed measures there were always air raid marshals patrolling the streets and their shouting *"lights out"* could be heard every evening.

***

During the last two weeks before Karl left for camp the inevitable happened. The last male teacher in Karl's school had been drafted and female teachers took over. Most of them came from the countryside where they had been teaching integrated classes.

The first few weeks were a time of adjustment for the boys. A female authority figure was as good as unknown. It was only the instilled obedience which prevented an out-and-out rejection.

In Karl's class there was an additional element of open abhorrence. Due to their age group they were now all members of the Jungvolk, where they had been taught that a German woman would never wear lipstick. The word 'makeup' had not been invented. Lipstick was supposedly a French invention and any woman who would wear lipstick was simply a whore. The squad leaders were unwavering in their teachings that women who *paint* their faces did so for the express purpose of attracting men and selling their bodies to them.

So far so good. Karl's mother did not own lipstick and Karl did not know of any women who would *paint* her face.

However, some of the female teachers who came from the countryside and small villages were for the first time in Berlin and thought that they had "*arrived.*"

It was a time of changing values in more ways than one.

Adults spied and reported on each other.

Children turned in their parents.

Relatives and friends disappeared during the night.

The Gestapo and the SS were hunting down people of different belief systems or social values.

And Karl's class in the elementary school of the Pfalzburger Strasse had a new teacher who was a whore. No doubt about it. Everybody could see it. The female teacher was wearing lipstick. Her name was Frau Kessel. The first time she entered the classroom the boys were stunned in utter disbelief.

When Frau Kessel told the class to sit down the boys simply walked out. They went home to tell their parents what was happening in their school.

Two days later all the boys were back in class. The school principal had instructed Frau Kessel to clean her face but the damage was done. The boys could see that their teacher was not a whore anymore but they knew that she had been one. The principal addressed the class and explained and talked, then talked and explained some more but he missed an entirely different point.

There was no way that the boys could conceive that a person, man or woman, who thought so little of their own face that they had to paint it, could possibly teach them anything of value.

Then the unthinkable but true happened. The principal dismissed all the women teachers who had shown up with lipstick on their faces and replaced them with *unpainted* female teachers from other districts.

Since Karl knew he only had to endure the female teacher for a few days, he was not as upset as some of his classmates. He was more amused than dismayed. In his mind Frau Kessel looked like a clown. Maybe not a happy clown, but a clown nevertheless.

On the day that his class walked out of school he visited his grandfather once more.

"Opa, you will not believe what happened." Karl wanted to know what his grandfather thought of the clown teacher. He thought that the old man might be laughing with him and was surprised by his opa's attitude.

"Karl, I hoped that my lesson of last week would have resulted in teaching you how to think correctly. Apparently you did not listen to what I told you."

"Sorry Opa, I will pay better attention. Promise." Karl was a little ashamed of his behavior.

"Alright, Karl, let us do this differently. I will ask you some questions. You are only allowed to answer yes or no." His grandfather sat down by the kitchen table and indicated to Karl to sit opposite from him. His grandfather looked Karl sternly in the eyes.

"Here it goes, Karl, I want fast answers. We are talking about the Frau Kessel. Based upon the teachings from your squad leader, did you believe that she was a whore?"

"Yes," answered Karl.

"Do you know that she is a whore?"

"No," Karl was getting the drift.

"Do you believe that a female teacher cannot teach you anything?"

"Yes," Karl answered a little slower.

"Do you know if a female teacher is able to teach you anything?"

"No," Karl understood now but his grandfather was not done.

"One more question, Karl. Do you understand that your belief system can be in conflict and even the complete opposite from what you know?"

"Yes, Opa, I understand." Karl liked his grandfather's simple lessons. He wished that his teachers would make learning this easy. Nevertheless he had a question of his own.

"Excuse me, Opa. Are you saying that I should only act on what I know and not according to my belief system?"

"See, Karl, there is already a conflict between the belief system and the knowing; not only within you but between the whole human race. Most, if not all of the wars ever fought, were based on either revenge or different belief systems."

Karl's grandfather got up to pour himself a glass of water from the faucet. "Listen Karl," he continued. "This is a subject I would like to debate with you when you reach mental maturity."

"When is this, Opa? You mean when I am an adult?"

"No, Karl, you are an adult when you reach physical maturity. I know many adults who are not mentally mature." He wanted to add that Karl's mother was one of them but he did not wanted to hurt Karl's feelings.

"For you, and for now, it is important that you understand and know the difference between right and wrong and act accordingly."

There was so much more he wanted to tell Karl about the many differences between knowing and believing but he did not want to confuse him. He himself had a hard enough time comprehending the forced belief system of the Nazi movement and the changes it caused. But he looked forward to debating this subject with Karl in a few years from now. He knew that the boy would apply what he learned and that the debate would be interesting

"Thank you, Opa. I will see you in six months from now." Karl got up with a heavy heart. It would be so nice if he could talk with his grandfather more often.

When he got home he saw that his mother was busy marking his clothing with a water proof laundry pen.

SIX

Karl's travel destination was the seaside resort Heringsdorf on the island of Usedom by the Baltic Sea. The Berlin school authorities chartered a riverboat with the name of Wintermaerchen (Winter tales), which traveled from a pier in the Havel River by Berlin through the Havel-Oder Canal and then downstream on the Oder river to Stettin. The island of Usedom was then reached by steamboat to the town of Swinemuende.

The day before the departure, Karl had to visit the local HJ office to obtain last minute instructions. The remainder of the day was filled with the packing and re-packing of two suitcases. Karl's mother had so much clothing laying on the beds and chairs that it would have taken five koffers (suit cases) to transport all of it.

When Karl's father arrived home from work in the evening, Karl had unpacked his cases for the third time. "Papa, help me. I am going bonkers with all this stuff." Karl was standing in socks and a turnhose (gym shorts) helplessly in front of the disorder on the bed. His brother did not help at all by sitting on the bed and throwing Karl's clothing willy-nilly in the air.

Herr Veth did not waste any time.

"Uniform?"

Karl had two matching summer uniforms and was required to wear one during the trip. He handed his father the other one.

"Next, sport shirts."

Karl had about five and his father packed three of them on top of the uniform.

"Next, shorts and regular underwear."

Within no time at all Herr Veth had finished packing the first suitcase. In the meantime, Karl's mother came to the rescue and packed the other suitcase with a pair of turn (running) shoes, socks and the remainder of underwear. There was even some room left for

Karl's favorite books. This was actually the whole dilemma in his previous packing efforts. He did not give a hoot about his underwear or the new swim shorts. It was his books that gave him problems. He needed the HJ manuals and instruction books, so they had to come along. Next he did not need, but wanted, the advanced school books for all the remaining grades up to the final school year. This amounted to a whole bunch. When his parents had realized how serious Karl was in his effort to enter the Napola they bought every school book available.

Karl's father came through again. "Your German grammar is excellent. You might need one dictionary for your writing. Your arithmetic is also outstanding. Take one book for algebra. History is your favorite subject, so take one you have not read. That's all. Write me if you need any of the remaining ones and I will send them to you. Your birthday is coming up in July and next week I will send you a pre-birthday present in the form of some University entry level books. You once told me that you like to study law. Is this still of interest to you?"

Karl looked at his father and wondered when he had slipped up. He did not remember when he had this conversation with his father but he had to agree that the laws of different countries were of great interest to him.

"Yes, Pappa, I know a little bit about German law. I also read a book on British law. But my real interest is in international maritime law."

Herr Veth looked at his son in surprise. This really was news to him. He did not even know that there was such a thing as maritime law.

"Alright, if I find something of this subject I will send it to you."

He closed the cover of the second suitcase.

"Now make us proud of you. I know that you will write for the HJ and the Jugendburg (school periodical); but these are monthly publications and I can pick up a copy at the school. Just don't forget Mutti and your brother and sister and me. We will cherish every one of your letters." He wiped a tear from his eyes. "Be a role model, Karl. But most of all be good."

He went to bed because he had to leave for work early in the morning.

When Karl went to bed he could hardly sleep. The excitement of leaving home and traveling with a group of children to an unfamiliar destination was one thing. Saying goodbye to his parents was another and he loved his little brother and his sister.

The worst was still ahead of him: saying goodbye to his mother. He tried not to think of it and wondered if he had made the right decision, but sooner or later he would have to leave home anyhow. *"Might as well get used to it early on,"* he thought by himself.

***

The next morning was a beautiful day. Spring was coming and the bright and almost warm sun chased last night's doubts from his mind. On the evening before, his mother had taken his sister and brother to the grandparents and was now traveling with him on the city train to Tegel where the river boat waited on the pier.

There were over 200 children crying and saying goodbye to their parents. Karl was not sure who cried the most. It was a toss-up between the adults and the kids.

There were also several boat workers who loaded the luggage on handcarts and rolled them into the freight room of the riverboat. This again caused a certain panic because some of the parents had no name tags attached to the baggage.

On this particular trip all of the children were between 8 and 9 years old and belonged to the Berliner school district of Kreuzberg. Karl knew the subway station of the area but that was about all. His luggage was already on board. As he stood next to his mother under the large sign marked "V" for the first letter of his last name he saw Rudy walking up to him. The squad leader was relieved when he spotted him. He shook hands with Karl's mother and then slipped a white and red armband over Karl's arm sleeve.

"Unterfuehrer" (sub leader) it proclaimed in big black letters.

"Say goodbye to your mother. I will console her. We need you to board the ship to instill order among the kids. You are the only sub leader we have on this trip and the teachers will be happy to see you. Do it now." He urged as he saw some hesitation on Karl's part.

Karl was happy to be forced to say a fast goodbye. He kissed his mother's tears away and closed his arms around her. "I love you Mutti. I will be back in six months," he whispered in her ear and then disentangled himself from her arms. He snapped a salute at Rudy and walked with firm steps toward the boat.

Before he entered the gangway he turned around and waved to his mother and then snapped his sharpest salute in the direction of a small musical band of World War One invalids who played the German farewell song: *"Muss I denn aus dem staedeli hinaus."* His salute was answered with a rousing shout of "Heil Hitler," though he thought that he heard someone yelling *"go to Hell,"* but he might have been mistaken. He could not discern his mother in the crowd, so he turned and entered the lower deck of the double deck boat.

As soon as he walked between the rows of crying and shouting children sitting on benches across the width of the ship he was discovered by a female teacher. "Over here, sub leader" she shouted in a warm voice and pointed to a seat next to the ship's window. Karl was amazed that his name and designation was on a card pinned to back board of the seat bench.

"Does every child have their name on a seat?" he asked the teacher, who had a plain but friendly face. No lipstick. She looked older than his mother, which in his mind made her old.

"No, only the teachers have a reserved seat. My name is Frau Niehaus." She offered Karl a handshake.

"My name is Karl Veth," Karl introduce himself. Frau Niehaus smiled.

"I know," she said pointing to his name on the seat. "You are the only sub leader on board." She wanted to say more but a squeaky loudspeaker announced that all the children were on board and departure was imminent. "We need to calm the children here on the lower deck. There are two more teachers on the upper deck so we don't need to go up there. However, your armband allows you to go wherever you please." She was interrupted by the ships horn which bellowed three times and Karl could feel a rumbling below his feet as the boat backed off from the pier. Frau Niehaus went to the rear part of the ship and motioned Karl to go to the forward section.

He strained once more to see his mother among the throng of people on the shore but gave up when he realized that there were just too many hands waving, which made it impossible to recognize an individual face. He thought about his task on hand and was glad that he had one. It kept his mind occupied. He went from row to row and noticed that the seats on the windows were ruled by the physically strongest children while the seats in the center of the boat were occupied by the more orderly ones.

As he came near the front of the boat he saw a boy quietly crying to himself. Karl could clearly see that all the other children had stopped crying and were busy talking to their friends but this little guy apparently had no one to talk to.

"Where are your friends?" Karl looked at the name tag dangling from the neck of the boy. "Where are your friends, Helmut?" He repeated. Helmut looked up at Karl.

"Home," came the answer.

"Do you know anyone on this boat?" Karl wanted to know. The boy shook his head. Karl looked at the identification tag once more and noted that the boy was nine years old and from a different school than the other kids. *This is odd* he thought to himself. "Helmut, you come with me," Karl decided to take this up with Frau Niehaus.

Karl took Helmut by the hand and led him to his reserved window seat. "Look out of the window, Helmut. Have you ever been on a ship before?" Helmut shook his head. "Good, that makes two of us. If you see something interesting come and tell me about it."

Helmut kneeled on Karl's seat and eagerly scanned the countryside. Karl patted the boy's back and went to find Frau Niehaus. He found her in conversation with another woman teacher near the staircase to the upper deck and told her about Helmut. The other teacher, Frau Seeger, seemed to be younger than Karl's mother and listened to Karl's report.

"Good work, Karl. I will pick up Helmut and take him upstairs with me. I have a nice seat up front and will share it with him," Frau Seeger said. Karl was impressed by the two women teachers. He could not imagine that a male teacher would have been more friendly or helpful.

Frau Niehaus told him that they had to go further to the rear of the boat to pick up sandwiches for the boys. The sandwiches had been prepared by a kitchen staff. They turned out to be simple grey rye-bread margarine sandwiches without any toppings or fillings. The treat was more than welcome and the boys wolfed them down. There were no complaints. None of the children were spoiled. Karl inquired if there were more sandwiches in case someone was still hungry and wanted a second one. He was assured that there were plenty more.

The ship was nearing the first of the three locks they had to pass on their trip to the Ostsee (Baltic sea) and everyone was crowding the windows. Karl marveled at the structure of the lock which was explained to the boys by a crewman.

After they had passed the lock, Karl noted again that the stronger boys controlled the access to the windows. It bothered him that the younger ones did not even have a chance to look out. He counted 12 rows of seat benches and had an idea. Frau Niehaus had emphasized to him that he was in charge of maintaining order and Karl dared to test his authority. It was kind of a rush for him because he had no experience in handling unruly children.

"Here goes nothing," he thought to himself as he climbed on top of a seat bench to make himself heard. He was right. Nobody listened to him. He climbed down again and decided not to go to Frau Niehaus for help. Instead he went to find the crewman who had given the information about the lock. He found him in the engine room and explained to him what he had in mind.

"You want to rotate the access to the windows?" laughed the crewman. "Will never happen, my boy. As long as I have been here the weak and polite ones sit in the middle. Don't even try. You will have all the bullies against you."

"Never mind that," said Karl. "Can you blow a whistle so that the children will listen to me?"

The crewman laughed again. "Yes, I will do that. Give me five minutes and I'll be there. But, I tell you right now, you can talk all you want. It will not happen."

Karl was not discouraged. He went back and walked the length of the seat benches. When he came to the windows he copied the names and birth dates of the most unruly ones. The boys glared for a brief moment at him and his uniform but respectfully made room for him when he pretended to catch a look out of the window.

"Now?" asked the crewman when he showed up next to Karl.

"No," answered Karl, "change in plans. May I please borrow your whistle?"

The crewman laughed again. "Good Luck." He handed Karl his whistle. Karl climbed once more on top of the bench and blew the whistle so hard that he almost scared himself. He had to blow it once more but then he had the attention of the boys.

"My name is Karl. I am the one to see when you are hungry. Did you enjoy your sandwich?" he asked.

There was some cheering from the boys and he blew the whistle again.

"Please hear me out. When we get to Heringsdorf we will have plenty to eat. Some of you will turn ten and will join the Jungvolk. I will call out the names of the few of you who are now eligible to assist me."

There was not even a murmur anymore. Everyone wanted to hear the names.

"Gert Wiesegang."

"Here," answered one of the intimidators." It was exactly the answer Karl had hoped for.

"'Here' is no answer for a German boy!" He thundered at the top of his lungs. The correct answer is PRESENT. If I hear anyone answering with 'here' he will be placed on probation." He faced the bully who was almost his size. "Once more, Gert Wiesegang!"

"Present!" The answer was loud and clear.

"Step forward into the center walkway."

Karl continued to call out the names. When he came to the end of the list he had ten bullies lined up in front of him.

"Listen up," he addressed them. "You are now my deputies. You will keep this position unless you fail to carry out my instructions."

He studied the boys in front of him. "You are a sorry bunch. Stand at attention when I speak to you" He stepped down from the bench and showed the boys how to stand at attention.

"You will start your duty right now. I want you to make sure that every one of the boys on this boat has equal time to sit at the window. You will rotate the boys every ten minutes. Not more, not less. Use the ship's clock to correctly time the intervals. If I catch you playing favoritism you will be dismissed and ineligible for leadership during the next six months. Get started."

The selected boys tried to salute, but Karl waved them off. "Later," he said, "we will have time for proper instructions. Right now carry out your assignment."

To the crewman's amazement the former disorderly boys marched now down the aisle, each one of them was pulling one of the shy kids along and allowing them to sit by the window.

"If I did not see it I would not believe it. Keep the whistle," he told Karl. "I have another one."

Karl went back to Frau Niehaus who had followed Karl's actions. "This was incredible. We were never able to control the window seats. Whoever appointed you as a sub leader must have known what he was doing. Very well done, Karl." She patted the seat next to her. "Sit down, Karl. Tell me, what did you mean by placing the boys on probation?"

Karl wrinkled his forehead. He was trying to remember what he had said. He gave up. "I don't know. I heard the word once and thought it sounded threatening. It worked, didn't it?" Frau Niehaus laughed, but stopped when she saw some hurt in Karl's eyes.

Karl got up again and repeated his maneuver on the upper deck with the same results, except that the third teacher, also a woman who looked ancient to Karl, took him to the side and called him a Nazi boy.

Karl took it in stride. "You instill order your way and I do it my way. However, I did not notice that your way ensured the smaller boys a seat by the windows."

"They are not sitting in the center forever. It is only a two day trip," asserted the teacher.

"Right," said Karl, "this is another reason why everyone should have an equal chance to enjoy the once in a lifetime trip."

"Dumb kid," the teacher had to get the last word in. "What do you know about once in a lifetime trips?"

Karl just turned away.

SEVEN

To Karl's satisfaction there was not even the slightest difficulty during the remainder of the day. His "deputies" not only assured an orderly exchange of the window seats, they also followed Karl's instructions and assigned rotating "clean up" squads to keep the aisles spotless.

Karl was unyielding in his demand that his deputies assigned the oldest and the strongest children to the cleanup detail.

"We need the older boys to act as a role model for the younger ones." Karl explained.

By 3:00 PM they had passed the last lock and at 5:00 PM the ship tied up to a landing on the Oder River. The boys disembarked and marched to a school in the small river village. Karl's simple idea of putting several boys in charge produced a small marvel of discipline. He had told his deputies to march the boys in proper formation and when he saw that the small local school had arranged for a field kitchen with a huge kettle of soup, he lined up the boys in two single-file lines to receive their rations.

The night was spent in the auditorium of the school. The boys slept under blankets on top of grain bags filled with straw. Karl had no clue where the teachers slept.

When sunrise came some local farmers showed up with sandwiches. By 8:00 AM the riverboat continued its journey to Stettin. They arrived in the early afternoon and everyone transferred to a larger steamboat to cross the bay to Swinemuende. It was a short trip of about two hours. After a march of another hour and a half, the boys arrived in the small village of Ahlbeck where they stayed overnight in a very comfortable boarding house. The suitcases of the children had been picked up from the ship by a few horse-drawn ranch wagons.

Early in the next morning they marched another two hours and arrived in Heringsdorf, their final destination. The seaside resort was originally a small fishing village but since about 1850 it was slowly developing into a luxury resort. Karl was somewhat familiar with its history and remembered that two Emperors of Germany had spent their summer holidays in this village. One of the Emperors was Kaiser Wilhelm II, but he could not remember the name of the second one. This part of history was not taught since Hitler had been in power. He had informed the German school authorities that all that "old stuff," as he called it, was not necessary to remember. He declared that history was being made now, by him, Adolf Hitler.

He had instructed the schools to dismiss the old history books and replaced them with up to date military reports describing every instant of the current war. The children had to learn and recite the time tables of the different battles, the commanding officers and other pertinent details.

It was only because Karl liked to learn about history that he had studied some discarded history books and therefore knew something about the island of Usedom and the Imperial bath houses in Heringsdorf.

Karl had been instructed by Rudy to report to the local HJ office. While Karl took these instructions seriously he also took them with a grain of salt. He figured that his first obligation was to his parents and not to the HJ. His first stop was to the local post office where he sent a letter to his parents and another one to his grandparents. They were not long letters. He had penned them while sitting in a center seat on the ship while he gave his window seat to one of the younger children. The letters were already sealed and stamped and he merely wrote *arrived safely* on the back of the envelope when he posted them.

The local HJ office, which doubled as the Jungvolk, informed him that due to his position as a subleader of a KLV camp he had been promoted to Jungschaftsfuehrer, the leader for the smallest and lowest unit in the Junkvolk. He was also told that if he performed as required he would receive another promotion after his six-month stint.

The leader of the local office wanted to know if Karl desired to attend classes in the village school. At first he did not understand but then it made sense to him. He was now almost 12 years old and the teachers in the camp would be conducting classes for the 8- and 9-year-old children. On first impulse he wanted to reject the local school because he believed that he knew already the course material due to his studies for the Napola but then he remembered his grandfather's lesson. While he *believed* that the village school could not teach him anything new, he realized that he did not *know* it.

Before he left the office, Karl asked the HJ leader for the directions to the school and presented himself to the principal. He was a nice white-haired gentleman. Karl guessed that he was at least 60 years old. The principal studied the copies of Karl's report card and scratched his head.

"It seems that you are somewhat advanced for our school. If you come back next Monday morning, I will arrange a test equal to our graduation test." He turned around on his Drehstuhl (swivel chair) and took some books from a shelf, which he handed to Karl. Here is something to read up on. They will help you to prepare."

Karl reached enthusiastically for the books. He had never encountered a book in which he had not learned something new or of value. Sometimes it was a subject he knew little about, sometimes it was a single sentence. But every time he read a book he was rewarded with a new or better understanding.

"Thank you Herr…" There was no name shield on the desk.

"My name is Groneberg," said the principal.

"Thank you, Herr Groneberg." Karl pressed the book under his arm. He was happy that he had decided to visit the school. If nothing else he had now some new books to digest.

The boys who had been on the ship were sheltered in two boarding houses. Karl was assigned with 95 children to a home bordering the dunes. He shared his bedroom with seven other boys. The Baltic Sea was about 200 feet from his bedroom window and the boys enjoyed listening to the gentle slapping of the waves at night. The instruction manuals he had received from Rudy called for the implementation of an activity plan. They gave no examples and Karl deduced that the reason for the missing activity plan or examples was probably due to the fact that the HJ had none.

He was right. The KLV camp in Heringsdorf, a resort village, was the first camp of its kind. It was 1942 and there had been only a few voluntary camps in existence. They were mostly on working farms where the boys were required to assist the farmers with their daily chores. These KLV camps served actually a dual purpose. Most, if not all, of the farm workers had been drafted and the work was piling up for the farmer. The boys were a welcome help and at the same time they were safe from the air attacks. In a sense Karl was a trial run for the KLV administration.

All of the activity plans Karl initiated had to be reported to the KLV and the HJ headquarters in Berlin. Many of his plans were later adopted as examples or became mandatory. Karl was keenly aware of the emphasis the HJ placed on physical education and activities and he was not about to let his personal preferences for academic studies interfere with his task.

But first he conferred with Frau Niehaus and Frau Seeger as to their school plan. He wanted to be mindful of the hours the boys were already occupied. He did not bother to consult with the third teacher who made a point of avoiding him. He did not even know her name. Besides, most of the time she seemed to be sleeping. Frau Niehaus was in charge of his facility and Frau Seeger was in charge of the other rooming house.

Karl's first questions concerned Helmut. The little boy without friends and from a different school district was on Karl's mind and he was kind of leaning on Frau Seeger to find out about it.

Then he started to develop his first activity plan with something obvious. At least it was obvious for him and became mandatory in all camps the moment he reported it to Berlin.

He initiated a 'Letter to Home' hour. Twice each week, for one hour at a time, he required that the boys write a letter home. He helped the boys by posting writing subjects on a blackboard. Topics ranged from the food they ate, descriptions of shells and other things they found on the beach, all the way to their physical activities. He also wrote on the blackboard a sample of the correct way to address an envelope. When he saw that a boy was struggling with the writing, he assigned one of his deputies to assist the 'partner'. In the beginning he addressed every one of the boys as 'partner' because he was unable to remember all their names. During the hours the boys were writing home he wrote the articles for the Jungvolk periodical and the school paper.

Karl's next activity item was also obvious. After all, the camp was on the Baltic Sea, so he initiated swimming instructions. He himself did not know how to swim and neither did any of the teachers. He solved this predicament by going to the HJ office and asking for help. Since the local boys were born by the sea, there was no shortage of instructors. Within a few weeks Karl knew how to swim. He liked it so much that he participated in all the water activities.

Two days after Karl had implored Frau Seeger to find out about Helmut, he had his answer. It turned out that on the day of their departure from Berlin there had been a second ship destined to the Baltic Sea. Both of the ships had the same name except that they were differentiated by the number 1 and the number 2.

Helmut, by some kind of error, had wound up on the wrong boat and his real destination was Ahlbeck. It was the village the boys had stayed overnight at on their march to Heringsdorf. Karl asked Gert- his strongest deputy- to assemble a team of six boys to walk Helmut to his real destination and also to carry his suitcases.

A little bit later Gert approached him in the dining hall. "I selected six boys, but two of them refuse to carry any suitcases. What do you want me to do?" Karl got up from his chair and blew the whistle. There were about 50 boys in the room from the second seating who now paid attention to him.

"I need six volunteers to carry two suitcases to Ahlbeck. You will leave early on Saturday morning. Before you return you are allowed one free hour to explore the village."

Karl could see more than ten hands in the air. "Make your selection," he said to Gert and sat down again. Frau Seeger showed up next to Karl.

"I think that I should go with them," she said. "Just to make sure they go to the right place and don't get lost."

Karl shook his head. "There is only a single road connecting us to Ahlbeck and they will not get lost in the small village. But if you insist, you better ask again for volunteers. I think that the boys raised their hand in anticipation of being alone on an adventure."

Frau Seeger seemed to mull this over in her mind. "I don't know Karl, maybe you are right. It is a longer walk than I wish to make anyway." She went back to her seat at the dining room table near the kitchen door.

In the meantime Karl read the books from Herr Groneberg to prepare himself for the Monday examination.

He had also learned from the local HJ office that there was some minor vandalism on the very old, nearly historical, entrance building to the old fishing pier. The local population blamed the newly arrived children for the damage, which consisted mainly of some scribbling on the wooden walls. Karl thought that this might have been possible during the few hours each day when the boys were free to roam along the beach. He also thought that this was a good enough reason to install some pre-Jungvolk training. He conferred with his team of deputies and initiated a guard detail.

The guard unit consisted of four boys who patrolled the entrance of the building. They were replaced every hour by another unit of four boys. There were no more reports of any misconduct and Karl speculated that the perpetrators might have been local boys who were not too fond of the newcomers. The former playground of a lonely beach was now pretty crowded with the boys from Berlin.

The transfer of Helmut to Ahlbeck went smooth without a hitch and without Frau Seeger.

***

Karl took the test in the local school and passed their graduation requirements without a glitch. Herr Groneberg, the principal of the school, invited Karl one afternoon to his home.

"I am sorry that our school is unable to provide any meaningful instructions for you. You exceeded our entire curriculum due to your studies for the Napola. I invited you to my house to tell you that I am glad that you did not get accepted." Karl was confused.

"Did I hear this right, Herr Groneberg? You are glad that I did not get accepted?"

"Yes, I assume that you know that the Napola is primarily teaching the gospel of the Nazi party."

Karl studied the face of the principal. He reminded him a little of his grandfather who had voiced a similar opinion. "No, Herr Groneberg. I applied because I was told that at least one of their schools teaches an advanced science program."

Herr Groneberg agreed. "Yes, there are currently 33 Napolas in Germany and I know that one of them is dedicated to the sciences. However, I am given to understand that some of their professors refused to join the Nazi party and have been dismissed." He looked at Karl. "Do you know what this means?"

Karl shook his head. "No, I don't know what this means."

The principal bent over his desk to make sure that Karl did not miss the meaning of his words. "It means that they will get arrested and placed into labor camps and the school will be taken over by members of the SS who will teach Nazi doctrines."

Karl understood what the principal tried to tell him, but he still had the words from his grandfather in his mind.

"Herr Groneberg, I appreciate what you are telling me and I

know now why you are glad that I did not get accepted." Karl stopped for a moment unsure how to proceed. "But, do you think that this will happen or do you know it?"

The principal was taken aback by Karl's question. He had thought that Karl was a bright boy and wondered if the kid was already brainwashed.

"No, Karl, nobody ever knows what will happen in the future. But based upon the current events, it is a given."

Karl thought before he voiced his next question. "Please tell me Herr Groneberg, is it not possible for me to just study and ignore the Nazi doctrine?"

The principal breathed a little easier. There was still hope for the boy. "Listen to me, Karl, for your own sake, listen to me. And always remember our conversation. You can believe all you want but," he looked deeply into Karl's eyes, "if you are long enough in the rain, you will get good and wet."

Karl was now sure that the principal was of the same mindset of his grandfather. He also liked that Herr Groneberg was using simple words. Words he could understand.

"Thank you Herr Groneberg, for inviting me to your home. I promise that I will remember what you told me." He turned to leave but turned around once more. "Is it alright if I come back to ask you more questions, Herr Groneberg?" The white haired principal smiled.

"You are welcome to visit me anytime. Karl. You know now where I live." Karl thanked him and left the modest house overlooking the beach. A few weeks later Karl learned that the principal had been arrested by the SS. He inquired at the HJ office about his whereabouts and was advised by the squad leader that nobody knew any details. Herr Groneberg had been a widower and lived alone.

After the six-month KLV term had passed, Karl returned to Berlin.

EIGHT

When Karl got back to Berlin he was allowed to stay home for a week before he had to go back to school. In the meantime, he decided to report to Rudy.

The location of the local Jungvolk and HJ headquarters had changed from the Wilmersdorf police station to Halensee (Burroughs in Berlin) but Rudy was still in charge of enrollment.

"I don't think that you will like what you see when you get back to your school," Rudy opinionated when Karl showed up.

"What has changed?"asked Karl.

"For one thing, all of the classes have been combined with a girl school from Wilmersdorf. For another, to prevent class sizes larger than 100 students, the school authorities decided to conduct the classes in two shifts which will alternate every week." Rudy reported.

"Two shifts? How will this work?" Karl asked, a bit bewildered.

"One week you will have classes from 8:00 AM to 1:00 PM and the next week your class will start at 1:15 PM and last until 5:30 PM," Rudy explained.

"Uff," answered Karl, "this does not sound too inviting." He pulled up a chair. "Anything else?"

Rudy reached into a drawer of his desk and handed Karl a large envelope stuffed with all kind of papers.

"There is plenty more. Your school building in the Pfalzburger Strasse will be taken over by the military. The changes will be initiated at the Brandenburger school. You will find all the details among those papers." Rudy pointed to the envelope in Karl's hand. "This should add about 15 to 20 minutes to your school walk," he guessed.

"Yeah, that's about right," agreed Karl. "Now, let me have the good news. I can see it in your eyes that you have more for me." He placed the envelope on the desk and readied himself for the next item on Rudy's list. The squad leader grinned at him.

"You are right. The good news is that you might not have to join your former classmates in the girly class. Due to your reports about your KLV camp and the various activities you initiated, you achieved something of an expert status. The school authorities intend to send you to the different camps to look at their conditions and report back to Berlin. In addition they also want you to address the parents here in Berlin and tell them about your camp experience." Rudy looked expectantly to Karl for his reaction. There was none. Karl sat bedazzled in his chair trying to comprehend what Rudy had told him.

"This should be the job of a teacher or at least an adult," he finally answered.

"Well," smiled Rudy, "that's where you are wrong. The school authorities think that the parents would like to hear from a student who attended camp and furthermore they have no adult to spare for this kind of thing. Do you know of a school principal with the name of Groneberg?" Rudy asked.

"Yes," said Karl, "he was the school principal on the Island of Usedom. Do you have any news about him? The last news I heard was not so good. I guess he has been arrested." Karl was excited to hear about him.

"Arrested? That's news for me," said Rudy. "All I know is that he sent a glowing report about you to the Berlin KLV headquarter. Is it true that you initiated cleanup details to assist the local merchants by scrubbing their sidewalks?"

Karl had to laugh when he saw the incredulous expression on Rudy's face. "What's the big deal about that? The sidewalks were always filthy with all the dog droppings. You should have seen the amounts of dogs in that village. Besides, the kids had enough time on their hands." Karl was proud of what he had done.

"But the kids," Rudy tried to imagine himself on his hands and knees and scrubbing dog poop off the sidewalk, "did they like it?"

Karl was amused by Rudy's expression on his face. "What is there not to like about it? The boys did not actually have to pick it up. The merchants gave them water buckets and hand brushes. The work detail consisted of five children and the camp had more than 200 boys. This meant that each boys turn was about six weeks apart. They were actually looking forward to it."

Rudy's face got even more disgusted. "They were looking forward to it?"

"Well, maybe that's a stretch but they received merit points which entitled them to a day off from school."

Rudy was still picturing himself scrubbing a sidewalk. "Karl, do me a favor and never, ever mention this work detail in one of our meetings here. Let this be just between you and boys from the camp and the school officials." He looked at Karl's uniform shirt. It was clean and freshly pressed. There was not a wrinkle on the chest or the sleeves. "Aren't you glad to be home again and have your mother washing your laundry and ironing your shirts?" he asked.

Karl grinned in return. "Yes, our laundry facility was not too great. But pressing my shirts? No, I learned to do this for myself and now my mother cannot do it well enough for me. I ironed this shirt myself last night."

Rudy gave up. He liked Karl, but now he thought that he had a neat freak in front of him. He wanted to tell him to get out and stay away from him when he remembered something.

"Karl, I almost forgot. Your friend Harold is back from the Napola. He reported to me last week."

"Harold is back? Do you know why?" Karl perked up. He had only received one short letter from Harold during the past six months while Karl had written to him several times.

"I think that he expected something else. When I asked him about the cadet school he answered that he would rather have a female teacher than Nazi instructors," Rudy remembered.

Karl snapped a salute and walked out. He went to his old school building in the Pfalzburger Strasse, which was in full swing of the transition. He could find neither a teacher nor a student. He did however read a notice on the principal's office that the KLV headquarters was now also transferred to the school in the Brandenburger Strasse. It was already late in the day and he decided to go home. He hoped that his father might be home early.

***

"I wondered when you would get here," his mother greeted him when he knocked on the door. "I cooked you your favorite pudding soup. Eat it before it gets cold. Pappa should be home any minute. He wants to talk to you."

Pudding soup was indeed Karl's preferred soup. He liked everything sweet. He had missed the soup in the last few months because the KLV camp woman who did the cooking thought that it was horrible to eat something sweet for dinner. Instead she served plenty of cabbage. Whenever the smell of the cooked cabbage penetrated the facility Karl ran away to the other house hoping that they served potatoes. Any potatoes, in any shape or form, were better than the floppy green leaves.

"Karl, we have to have a talk. Keep your seat at the table," Herr Veth announced after dinner. He took some blue letters from his briefcase. The blue envelopes indicated that they were sent from the school administration. "Frankly I am puzzled. The principal from your Pfalzburger school has been drafted but he is still available during the next week. He wants to meet with me and with you while he is still in charge of the school. According to his letter you passed some graduation tests in Usedom." Herr Veth looked up from the first letter. "You never wrote me about these tests. Why not?"

Karl moved around on his chair. "There was no reason for me. I passed some tests. That's all. There was nothing to write about." Karl added some explanations about why he took the tests in the first place.

Herr Veth listened while he sorted through the other communications he had received from the KLV headquarter.

"Well, Karl, it seems that the principal from Usedom was sufficiently impressed to send several reports to the KLV officials and now they also want to meet with us. Do you know what these meetings will be about?" Karl's father had a tight work schedule which did not allow him to take a day off but it looked like it could not be avoided. In any event, he wanted to be prepared for the meetings.

"Maybe it has something to do with the things I complained about to the KLV." Karl speculated.

"What did you complain about, besides the things you already wrote to me about?" Herr Veth was curious to know.

Karl had to think for a moment because there had been plenty and he only wanted to tell his father about the ones which had bothered him the most.

"Many of the 8-year-old kids did not have sufficient underwear. Our laundry facility could not keep up with the demand. Either we needed additional help or the children needed more clothing to tide them over between the wash days. Also, their parents need to write more often. You should have seen the disappointment in the faces of the kids during mail call. Some boys received a letter every week.

Some of the other ones waited every day for three weeks without so much as a postcard from home." Karl was still upset as he thought back.

"So, you reported to the KLV officials about parents who did not write to their children?" Herr Veth wanted to be sure that he understood correctly.

"Not at first," answered Karl. "When I saw the boys crying I started to write short postcards myself to their parents asking them politely to write to their children. Only when some of the parents ignored my cards did I report the situation to the school officials."

Karl's father considered the answer. "I would think that it would have been the responsibility of the teachers to report about these things."

Karl shook his head. "No, Pappa, I don't know, but I don't believe that teachers know what it feels like to be a kid and away from our parents. All they ever say is: '*Don't worry, your parents are alright. They will write when they get to it. Don't be such a Mamma's boy.*' I don't think that we need more caring adults in the camps, although it would help. I think that the parents should know that we feel terrible when some of our friends receive mail while we stand there helpless with empty hands."

Karl looked up to his father and when he received no answer he added: "The adults who dreamed up this idea of separating the children from their parents because of the air attacks were probably thinking correctly, but they missed explaining to the parents of the need to write. Because they missed it I took it on myself to report about it." Karl thought that he had done the right thing but was afraid that he had meddled into some adult behavior. "If they did not like what I conveyed they could have stopped me. The only answer I received was always the same: *Keep on reporting.*" Karl saw that his father was stuffing the letters back into his briefcase.

"Nothing to worry about, Karl. We go and see your principal tomorrow."

The night was interrupted by a three hour air raid and the Veth family took shelter in the basement of their apartment building. The air raid warden was controlling the orderly retreat of the tenants to the cellar and Karl was holding his little brother Willy close to him as they listened to the crackling of the exploding anti-aircraft shells. His father was sitting by his mother on a bench and his little sister was soundly asleep in the arms of her mother. Karl could not help but notice that this was one of the very few times the family had ever spent time this close together. He looked along the dirty basement hallway and saw that all the other families were also huddled together. While he wondered why none of the families spoke to each other, he fell asleep with his brother's head in his lap. When the all-clear signal sounded there was a sigh of relief among the tenants as they shuffled up to their apartments.

***

The meeting with the principal went totally different than Karl or his father had anticipated. The principal, Herr Nordweg, was not expecting them. The Veth family did not own a telephone and had not announced their visit. But, Herr Nordweg was none-the-less happy to see them. He made several phone calls and within a few minutes a soldier showed up announcing that he had a car waiting for them. This was the first time that Karl rode in a private car, other than a taxi cab, and he admiringly touched the soft seat cushions.

It was a very short ride to the Ferbelliner Platz where they entered a fairly new government building. It was built in the modern architectural style with grand tall entry doors topped by an imposing bronze eagle. Karl was duly impressed while his father did not pay any attention to the Nazi décor along the hallways.

They were led to a meeting room and within a few minutes they were seated among maybe 12 or more school and government bureaucrats. To Karl's astonishment, the presiding white-haired school administrator seemed to have all of Karl's letters to the KLV administration in front of him. There were also copies of the 'Jugendburg' and 'Hilf mit' school and Jungvolk periodicals which featured some of Karl's reports.

Herr Veth was impressed when he realized how much Karl had written within the six-month period.

Principal Nordweg opened the meeting by reading aloud each and every one of Karl's letters. In addition he read also the letters from principal Groneberg. When he was done he asked the group for comments.

"We should form a task force to deal with the individual problems,'" declared the top school administrator. "There seem to be many areas which obviously need improvement." While all of the officials agreed and asked for volunteers, Herr Nordweg addressed the meeting once more.

"Hold on, we can do this later. At this time I'd like to discuss the idea from principal Groneberg. He suggested that we should assign Karl Veth to visit various camps and to report back to us about their conditions as seen from the children's perspective. While this is a new and bold idea, we have to consider that within a few months from now the evacuation of our students will become mandatory." He wanted to add something but was rudely interrupted by an SS Lieutenant.

"Principal Groneberg was a traitor. He advised his students how to evade Junkvolk and HJ duties and he spoke out against our beloved Fuehrer Adolf Hitler..." He also wanted to say more but was interrupted by the school administrator.

"Where is Principal Groneberg? We have not heard from him lately. And, what are you doing here? I don't remember sending an invitation to SS officers."

The lieutenant did not back off. "I have been ordered to attend because we arrested your swine Groneberg. Before he was sent to hard labor he confessed that there are traitors in this school administration." He pointed to a teacher sitting at the far end of the table. "Herr Weinert, one of your teachers and a ranking member of our party reported your teachings to us."

He turned to face principal Nordweg. "How dare you declare openly that the evacuation of students will become mandatory? This is outright inflammatory. Have you not read and studied Herr Hitler's proclamation that we will employ wonder weapons? Even our beloved leader of the German air force, Hermann Goehring, has declared that the Berlin airspace cannot and will not be penetrated by enemy aircraft."

He walked to open the door and four more SS men entered the room. "I could arrest all of you. But for now, I only take this stinking weasel Nordweg with me. But I promise that I will be back." The four SS men formed a circle around the helpless principal and pushed him out of the room.

Before he left, the lieutenant turned to look at Karl. "Good writing, Jungschaftfuehrer. I read every one of your articles in the 'Jugendburg'. Keep it up, but beware of the traitors, they are all around you." He snapped a salute in Karl's direction which Karl did not return. He was too stunned that his principal had been arrested.

The school administrator got up from his chair and walked towards Herr Weinert, a member of his school board and now a disclosed Nazi member. "I would have never suspected that you informed on us. We are not conspirators. We are supposed to serve as an example for our students and we are supposed to protect them from harm. The arrest of principal Nordweg is a direct result of your ill-advised reports to the SS. Whatever happens to him is on your conscience. You are dismissed from the school board. Get out!"

Herr Veth wanted to leave the meeting but the school administrator needed his signature on a prepared document. It was in essence, consent from him as a parent to allow his son to undergo an elementary school graduation test. After Herr Veth signed the document, he asked when this test would be conducted.

The school administrator smiled. "Don't worry, Herr Veth. There will be no more tests for your son. He demonstrated to our satisfaction that he is capable to assist us with the school evacuation program. You should be proud of him."

He wanted to shake hands but Karl's father was confused. "If there are no more tests for Karl, why did you need my consent?" he asked.

"Just a formality, Herr Veth. We don't want you to come after us for interrupting your son's schooling. Believe me; he will learn more during the next two years than we could possibly teach him."

The old school official had no clue at that time how true his comments would turn out to be. Herr Veth wanted to finally leave but was still forced to wait for Karl, who could not get away. Every one of the teachers and officials had questions and suggestions for him and it took over another hour until Karl and his father were back on the street.

"What do you think, Pappa?" Karl asked.

"Think about what, Karl?"

"About the arrest of Herr Nordweg and of the meeting."

Herr Veth shook his head. "I don't allow myself to think about something until I have all the pertinent facts in front of me. But I surely learned something and I hope that you learned it too." He turned to Karl. "Guess what it is."

"Not to trust the teachers who might be Nazi members?" he ventured a guess.

"No, Karl, much too complicated. We should learn from this incident to keep our mouth shut. Let's see what will happen to the administrator. I hope that he did not make a mistake by throwing Herr Weinert out of the room."

Herr Veth was right. It was a mistake. The administrator should have kept his mouth shut.

Two months later the administrator was arrested. Nobody ever heard of any charges being leveled against him. All the school board heard was that he was awaiting trial in a concentration camp. He was temporarily replaced by Herr Weinert, who was shortly thereafter drafted into military service.

NINE

A few days later, when Karl attended the weekly Jungvolk meeting he saw Harold again.

"What happened at the Napola and why are you back in Berlin?" Karl wanted to know as they started walking home.

Harold answered with his typical grin. "Well, I really liked the discipline and the ambition of the students. There is not a single slacker or slob around. You would like it."

"Sounds inviting," remarked Karl. "What was it that you did not like?"

"Several things," answered Harold. "Most of all I did not like that we were manipulated to report about our relatives and parents."

"What do you mean by manipulated?"

"Well, first they asked us to name and list all our close relatives like uncles and grandparents. Then, a few days later we were instructed to write essays about their jobs and about their discussions and the discussions your parents had at home. If you failed to write about some relative whom you had previously mentioned, you were questioned about him."

Harold adjusted his belt buckle and Karl noticed that his friend had lost some weight.

"I don't understand why your teachers would be interested in your parents' discussions. It sounds like as if they wanted to learn from you, while it should be the other way around." Karl tried to make sense of what his friend told him.

"No, Karl, forget about your idea of a regular teacher. In the Napola we have no teachers like we do here in school. Instead, we have several different instructors." Harold was done with his belt and continued. "The assignments to write about our parents came from the 'Political Education' instructor. A young fellow with a 'party bonbon' on his jacket."

"How can you learn from a young fellow?" Karl wanted to know. "How old was he?"

Harold shook his head. "Karl you don't understand. Listen to what I am telling you. I use the word 'instructor' on purpose. Right in the beginning, during the first hour of our introduction, we were told to be absolutely precise in choosing our words to communicate. The word 'teacher' implies that you are being taught. The word 'instructor' does not apply to teaching. In the Napola we are being 'instructed'. A far cry from being taught. Think about it."

Karl allowed that there was a difference. "So, do you think about it a lot? I mean do you really think so deeply about the difference between being taught or being instructed that you are willing to give up the cadet school?" he wanted to know.

"No, Karl, I don't think too much about it but it bothers me. Matter of fact it bothers me a lot." The boys had walked from the Jungvolk assembly hall to the street corner where they usually parted. Karl had to turn into the Uhland Strasse while Harold went too far and had to double back.

"Let's turn around and talk some more," suggested Karl. "What else turned you off?"

Harold looked at his friend. "When I think about it, there was not much that I liked. On Sunday mornings we had to march around the local Catholic churches and sing at the top of our lungs. The purpose was to sing loud enough to interrupt the church service."

Karl was puzzled. "Did your instructors justify the interruption of the church service?"

"No, but that's not all," answered Harold. "We had to place one of our boys at the church portal to listen to what was going on in the church. When the ringing of the little bells at the altar announced the beginning of the Holy Communion, he waved at our drummers to step up to the entrance to beat double time. At the same time our trumpets repeated the attack signal over and over again."

"The attack signal," exclaimed Karl. "You were attacking the church members?"

"No, you dummy. We were not attacking anyone. It was just the loudest trumpet signal we knew. The trumpet detail, about 20 boys, rehearsed it every morning and every evening."

"So, the way I understand it, the whole exercise was for the express purpose to interrupt the service." Karl tried to sum it up.

Harold shook his head. "I think that there was more to it." He turned to look behind them just in case someone might be overhearing their discussion.

"When we blew the trumpets, some of the church members came out to complain..." He wanted to say more but was interrupted by Karl

"Do you blame them, Harold? I don't think that your parents would tolerate this disruptive exercise." Karl knew that Harold's parents were Catholic.

"No, let me finish, Karl. During this exercise we were escorted by civilian members of the Gestapo. As soon as a church member came out to complain he was interrogated by the Gestapo and warned that if he ever interrupted the musical exercises of the Napola again, he would be detained."

Karl was dumbstruck. "I heard that the Gestapo hunted down members of the Jewish faith. Are you telling me that they are now after the Catholic faith too?"

"I don't know that, Karl, but I heard that they are after any and all dissidents. I have the strange feeling that they singled out the women. I overheard that they are running short of labor in the ammunition and armament facilities."

"What about the men?" Karl inquired.

"I heard them say not to worry about the men because they would soon enough be drafted into the Reserve Defense Divisions."

"What are the Reserve Defense Divisions?"

"We were told that during the next few months the draft for the military service will be extended to include every able man, including the previously exempt occupations."

Karl thought that he had heard enough. The boys had walked in a circle around an apartment block and he needed to get home.

"Harold, how about discussing what you just told me with my grandfather? When do you need to report back to the Napola?"

"I have at least another week. The introduction period is over. I applied for a crash course in the English language, which I'd like to attend and I have to wait until I am accepted."

"Yes," Karl agreed. "I would like to learn another language too. It would be nice if we could study together. If you do take the course, when will you be back?"

"I don't know. I think that it will be another six months." Harold pointed at a street car going by. "There, have you noticed that all the formerly male street car attendants have been replaced with women?

Before I left for the Napola I did not see a single one. It looks like the final draft has begun."

Karl wanted to answer when he noticed Rudy walking down the street towards them.

"I just received a notice that we are supposed to help some fertilizer farmer in Plaue on the Havel River. Since none of you has to be back in school I expect you tomorrow morning at 9:00 AM sharp."

Karl nodded his agreement and then asked, "I thought that this kind of farm work was the job of the Reichsarbeitsdienst?" (Government labor service)

"Not anymore," answered Rudy. "The labor service is being discontinued. All the men are being drafted into the infantry and the women are being trained to be Flakhelfers. (Air defense helpers). In any event, it is now the job of the HJ to help the farmers. Technically, this excludes you because you are still in the Jungvolk. However, I am short of available members and it is only for one day." Harold did not even listen to the explanations of Rudy.

"Off course we will be in your office tomorrow morning. But how do we get to Plaue?" Karl wanted to know how he was expected to reach the small town outside of Berlin on the Havel River.

"I think that the farmer will provide transportation," guessed Rudy. Karl wanted to ask what kind of help was expected of them but Rudy had crossed the street to take a bus home.

"Do you know what a fertilizer farmer does?" Karl enquired of Harold. "No, not a clue. I just hope that it has nothing to do with cow manure." Harold had the uneasy feeling that they were being ordered to work with dung.

***

The next morning turned out better than the boys had expected. When they arrived at the office there was a bus waiting for them and a dozen HJ members to drive them to the farmer on the low land of the Havel River.

All of the boys were in uniforms and nervous about how they would look after they were done with the work. It turned out that they did not have to worry. It was actually a very clean job that awaited them. The farmer harvested the top layer of soil from the moorlands and sold it as fertilizer.

The boys' job consisted of laying a Knueppeldamm (placing strong branches) over the harvested area to provide something like a path through the boggy marsh. The only danger was that most of the watery area was down to a depth of eight to nine feet without a solid ground. If you slipped and fell in the morass, you could easily drown. Swimming was impossible and not an option.

The farmer took great care in explaining to the boys where not to step and how to lay the branches on top of each other.

"How do you navigate this swamp by night?" Karl asked.

"You don't," answered the rancher. "You will lose your direction due to the many lightening bugs. They will confuse you into thinking that you are close to a road or to a ranch. None of my family ever ventures out at night."

The HJ members worked a lot faster than the rancher had anticipated. He rewarded the team with a nice meal of fried potatoes and the boys were home before sunset.

The British planes attacked Berlin now more often. Shortly before midnight there was another air raid alarm. This time the whole cellar shook as the Veth family went below for protection. The vibrations were due to some air mines, which leveled an apartment complex around the corner. Right after the all clear signal sounded an air raid marshal solicited help from the tenants to dig through the rubble for possible survivors.

It was the first time that Karl smelled the stench of burnt human flesh and he got sick to his stomach. He wanted to chicken out of the gory labor by saying that he would get additional help from the HJ Dienststelle (HJ office), but when he saw that his mother was carrying the charred remains of a child to a nearby waiting truck, he decided to stay.

Everybody helped and he realized that his mother had an easy excuse to leave because of his little sister. Instead she put his five year old brother in charge of his two year old sister and left them in the security of the apartment.

The digging out of casualties was a gruesome task which got no easier as the day came to an end. After the helpers moved the bodies to a Sammelplatz, (collection area), the grisly mission continued by trying to identify the individual corpses.

Many times they were unable to differentiate between the male and the female casualties and any personal identification was nearly impossible. Neither Karl nor any of the other helpers realized at that time that this was actually a benign chore compared to what lay ahead of them.

It was benign because the air raid had stopped and the helpers could concentrate on nothing else but on the work at hand. In the following months these jobs became extremely difficult because continued bombing hampered and constantly interrupted rescue efforts.

The few civilian authorities who were still working decided to tally the survivors instead of counting the dead. Finally, during the last few weeks, before the surrender of Berlin to the Soviet forces, any and all rescue attempts came to a complete stop. While the allied planes bombed from above, the Soviet artillery hammered Berlin nonstop.

In spite of all the civilian casualties, the authorities of Berlin never ordered the population to evacuate. Hitler was adamant in his final order of "Scorched Earth." Scorched Earth was all he wanted his enemies to find.

Within two days after the mass burial of the unidentified casualties, the survivors of the apartment house scratched their names on the larger pieces of the rubble. They also put the current date behind their names. This way it was clear to anyone who might be searching for them that on this date they were still alive.

TEN

"Tell me about your experience in the Napola," Karl's grandfather prompted Harold when the boys visited him.

"There was not much of an experience," answered Harold. "We were awakened with a trumpet signal at 6:00 AM. After about an hour of Fruehsport (early morning exercise), we ate breakfast. Then began the school hours which during the time I was there consisted of nothing but somehow convincing us that we were part of the foundation of a 1,000-year empire."

"Were all of your teachers civilians or were there also some in uniform?" Karl's grandfather asked.

"Some of them were in SS uniforms but most of them were civilians. However, all of them were wearing the party emblem."

"What did they mean by a 1,000-year empire?" Karl was eager to hear the answer.

"I am not too sure, because we were not allowed to interrupt the instructors with questions. But from what I could gather, they meant that all the previous empires failed to maintain longevity by deterioration from within."

"And the Nazis have a structure in mind to avoid the pitfalls," Grandfather guessed.

"Yes," answered Harold. "The idea is to build a race with strong everlasting principles. We, the graduates of the Napola, were selected because of our heritage and our demonstrated ambitions and we were to be trained to be the leaders of this nation."

Karl wanted to ask a follow-up question but was interrupted by his grandfather. "Did they explain why in their effort to build a 1,000-year empire, they were persecuting people of different faiths?"

"Not so much of a different faith, but by citing examples of how to recognize inferior people." Harold warmed up to the subject.

"So, the builders of this empire pursue and hunt down the

Gypsies and the Jews for the solitary reason that they are inferior to the Aryan race?" The grandfather doggedly steered his questions in the direction he wanted to go.

"No, Herr Veth," answered Harold. "None of my instructors ever directly mentioned a Jew or a Gypsy. However, they did say that homosexuals should not be permitted to live because they are mentally deranged and even if they could reproduce, they would produce nothing but other deranged and mentally ill individuals."

"So, then I take it that the goal of the Nazi's is to eliminate all mentally unbalanced members of society." The WW I veteran tried to sum it up. "If this is the case," he continued, "then why are they after the Jews? I have met quite a few of these people during my lifetime and none of them were mentally challenged. Did your instructors bother to explain this?"

Harold tried to remember, but he was unable to recall a direct mentioning of any particular race. "No, however, they instructed us how to discern unproductive tendencies and shirkers of honest labor."

"I'd like to hear more about that," the old man encouraged.

"Well, for one thing, you recognize a drifter by seeing that he never learned a trade, that he does not belong to a recognized trade guild and is therefore a master of nothing."

"This is nonsense," interjected Karl. "We have extremely knowledgeable minds in the sciences- in astronomy, in physics, in the mathematical sphere, in the medical field and in a long list of other occupations. None of them belong to a trade guild! Besides, what about all the military leaders and achievers?"

Harold was undaunted. "I said already that we were not allowed to ask questions. We were, however, told that the elimination of the drifters was only the beginning to rid the nation of unproductive elements. The next wave would be the elimination of unproductive intellectuals and disloyal civil and military administrators." He hesitated for a moment before he proceeded.

"As for the scientists, we were told that they need to become members of the Nazi party. If they object they will also be eliminated. Our country does not have the resources to support slackers or nonconformists. They will no longer be tolerated. This is also the underlying reason to report any subversive conversation of our parents or relatives."

Karl was getting upset and walked back and forth in the living room, but the grandfather remained stable. "There is nothing really new about the heavy handed enforcement of the rules by the rulers. The history is rich with examples. However, what bothers me is that Hitler is encoding the minds of children. If they don't learn how to tell the difference between good and evil, I don't want to be around when they become adults. The whole country will experience a rude awakening."

"They are not conditioning me," objected Karl, sitting down again.

"Maybe yes and maybe no, just remember what I told you about being long enough in the rain." Karl's grandfather was visibly worried. "Just listen to the way your friend tells us about his indoctrination. If I did not know him, I might already suspect that he is a little programmed."

Harold thought again before he spoke. "I have to agree with your grandfather, Karl. He is right about the rain. This is the very reason that I want out of the Napola, before I am getting good and wet. I, for one, did not study to become all of a sudden brain-dead."

While Harold defended himself, the grandfather wanted to hear some more examples of how the teachers programmed the students.

"I heard some stories against advertising. Did your instructors have anything to say about that?" he pressed Harold.

"Yes," answered Harold, "I remember one of the SS instructors who told us that advertising was a hoax invented by the Jews. He explained it this way: If you have something of value to sell then you don't need to advertise it. All you have to do is state what it is and then name your price. And once you name your price it is not subject to any negotiations. He told us that all of the drifters, nomads and gypsies are schacherers (dealers). They name a price but fully expect to deal. This is in strict violation of the German law."

The grandfather had to agree that even under Prussian law it was strictly forbidden to negotiate for a price. Going all the way back to 1772 when the Kingdom of Prussia was founded, any price negotiation was unlawful. This not only extended to the price but also to the hours allocated to the merchants.

Nobody was allowed to set their own business hours. Every merchant had to open and to close their business at strictly enforced Ladenschlusszeiten (business hours).

Even the lunch hours were regulated. From noon until 1:30 PM, all the stores had to be closed. The only exceptions were the newspaper vendors in the railroad station and the airport. The merchants were held responsible for any customer who remained on the premises after 12:00 noon. The customers could not be waited on and had to leave the store. Any merchant who was found to be in violation of this law was severely fined by the Gewerbepolizei (trade police). The fine ranged from monetary fines to revoking the business license.

The prices were set by the Gewerbeaufsichtsamt, the trade observation authority. If a merchant was found guilty of undercutting the competition, the penalties could be severe and ranged from losing the business license all the way to prison terms.

The old man knew that this had been a bone of contention ever since the Jewish traders started to open stores in Germany. They not only undercut prices but also sold items on credit. Hitler claimed that the practice of the Jewish jewelry stores and furniture dealers of selling their merchandise on credit led to the debt stricken public. He proclaimed that every citizen should only buy what he could afford. If he did not have the money to pay for the regulated price he should not enter the store in the first place.

The old war veteran had his own ideas why the public was indebted to merchants but this was not the subject of their conversation.

"I agree that the set prices should be observed. But did the instructor compare the merchandise advertising to the governmental propaganda? Did he even mention something in this regard?"

"Oh, yes, Herr Veth. There is a tremendous difference between advertising and propaganda. We received several lectures on this subject," Harold responded excitedly. "First of all, advertising is only needed if you desire a competitive edge over your competition. If every merchant sells the same butter for the same price then advertising is unnecessary. But if your advertising claims that you are the best butter dealer in Berlin or in a given territory, you are creating the impression that your butter might represent a better value for the money. Just to create the impression is most certainly against the law because the merchant who does not advertise is already thought of as inferior in his product. Our German laws assure equality for every merchant. That is also the main reason for uniform and regulated business hours"

Harold knew something about this subject because he had debated it with some of the other students. Karl, on the other hand, had never heard of a comparison between advertising and propaganda and was glued to his seat. His eyes told Harold that he wanted to hear more and Harold really went into gear.

"Every advertiser is a fraud because he creates an illusion and therefore he deserves to be arrested. He should be beaten and condemned to hard labor."

The old man looked at the boy and wondered if this was Harold's idea or if he had been already conditioned by the Nazi school.

"What is your personal take on this Harold?" he asked.

"My personal take? I think that an advertiser creates no value and is only self-serving. Now whether it is good or not, to be self-serving, I have not thought about. But, I do know that it is against our laws."

"Come on Harold, tell us how it differs from propaganda." Karl really wanted an answer from his friend.

"Your grandpa said already that propaganda is a governmental function. It has nothing to do with business. Furthermore, the government needs to bring its ideas across to the public and needs to resort to effective methods. Therefore, it encourages gifted speakers to explain the government plans. Besides that, the government is most certainly allowed to stick signs on billboards. Since the signs reflect the doctrine of the government it is not against the law."

"Harold, think about it. Are you saying that the government can proclaim whatever it wants because it makes the laws and therefore is able to get away with outright lies?" Karl's grandpa wanted to be sure that he understood what Harold had been taught.

"I don't know about outright lies, but yes, our government is allowed to make the laws. Therefore, it is able to proclaim or to deny without coming into conflict with the laws." Harold was unyielding.

The old man Veth nodded in agreement. "Alright, Harold, now think before you answer. Considering your previous point about advertising would you now come to the conclusion that the propaganda of our government is self-serving?"

Harold did not miss a beat. "Of course our government is self-serving. I don't think that there is any difference between our government and other governments. They are always self-serving."

"Then you don't even think about the fact that Herr Hitler can say what he wants, but that we citizens are in jeopardy if we don't agree with him." Herr Veth wanted to turn this conversation into a lesson.

Harold showed that he was indeed already too long in the rain. "No Herr Veth, Herr Hitler does not say what he wants. He is only taking measures to assure that we are building an eternal empire. It will last at least a 1,000 years because we will eradicate the mentally ill by not permitting them to reproduce and also by sterilizing their roots. We will also abolish any vagrants and quacks, regardless of their faith, by sending them to labor camps. If any nonproductive person does not like our restraints they are free to migrate to other countries, which will suffer by this fact and therefore will never be of any competition to our disciplined nation."

Karl was stunned by Harold's outpouring. "Harold, what is the matter with you? Don't you realize that you are sounding like a member of the Nazi party?"

Harold turned to face his friend. "No, Karl, I don't sound like a Nazi. Discipline and productivity are the hallmarks of our Prussian culture and upbringing. There is nothing wrong with it."

Herr Veth intertwined. "There is something wrong with using the Prussian discipline to control young minds. Herr Hitler is using the very core of our heritage by exploiting it and using it as a tool for his ambitions."

"Alright, maybe he is," allowed Harold. "But, if he is using it as a tool, and if he is not using it to create a pure and productive nation, then what exactly is he trying to achieve?"

Herr Veth felt challenged. "Herr Hitler is the very person he wants to eradicate. He might have started out with good intentions, but he is mentally unbalanced and now almost insane."

"Then how come he is loved by the whole nation?" Harold interjected.

"His first programs of building the Autobahn, of installing the Reichsarbeitsdienst (national labor service) were almost strokes of genius. This endeared him with our people suffering from unemployment. Then he promised things which he is unable to deliver. His hypnotic power as an orator causes the people to cheer. They don't love him. They are simply mesmerized by a charlatan."

The old man answered carefully. He was not sure of Karl's friend. It could very well be that the boy was spying for the SS.

"So, Opa, what do you think Herr Hitler's goals are?" Karl tried to follow the thinking of his friend but had a problem with the word sterilization. He did not know what it meant and he would have to talk to him when they were alone.

"I don't know what his goals are or what to think. All I know is what I see. We are assaulting other countries and forcing our belief system on other cultures. We invaded Poland and France and all of the lower countries and Scandinavia. We build bridges with the full intent of burning them by executing a non-aggressive agreement with the Soviet Union and then attacking them. Our troops are all the way into Africa and we are suffering casualties by the millions in addition to the millions we are killing in the name of war." His grandfather was again choosing his words carefully.

"There is no doubt in my mind that our country will suffer greatly from Herr Hitler's action. Our troops are already retreating in Russia. We are running out of food and material. The western allies will bomb our civilian population without mercy and bury us under the rubble of our cities."

Harold was trying to relate what he had been told at the Napola with what he just had heard. "There is the promise of the wonder weapons we are developing. What do you think about that, Herr Veth?"

The old man shook his head. "I heard the same stories and even know about our experiments with rocket propelled bombs and planes. However, even if we have the most advanced minds in Germany working on a wonder weapon, it cannot change the outcome." He got up from his chair to retrieve an atlas from the top of the living room cabinet. He opened a large map of Europe and pointed to the small country of Germany. "Here, see for yourself." He drew with his finger lines connecting Germany and all the occupied countries. He started in France and Belgium and then traced all of Scandinavia and going through Poland and Hungary far into Russia. "How do you suppose a wonder weapon would help to maintain our supply lines? Alone the logistics are against us and I cannot even show you on this map the position of our troops in Africa."

The boys were used to studying the advances of the German troops. It was the daily school subject of history. But no one had ever told them about the logistics of getting food, material, ammunition and replacements of vehicles and weapons to the front lines. Alone the comparison of the tiny outlines of Germany and the vast areas of the occupied countries spoke silently for the impossibility of the supply task.

"Don't forget," continued the retired cavalry officer, "our weapon manufacturing facilities are now also coming under the bombing attacks of the western allies."

"What about our allies?" asked Karl.

"Our allies?" the old officer laughed. "Now that is a joke. You are talking about the Italians, right? I think they are great artists and singers, but soldiers?" He shook his head. "No, I don't think so. However, the Japanese are a formidable force, but they have enough to do with the Americans. They are unable to supply us."

He took the atlas from the boys and got up.

"If you are able to come back tomorrow I will have something to show you."

The boys agreed to come back the next day and spent the rest of the day traveling the subway to the center of the city.

***

Karl wanted to see the area of the Tiergarten, a park in the city of Berlin, where the Jungvolk and the HJ was to practice as a human cordon to keep the masses of the population in check during an upcoming parade. It was supposed to be a mass demonstration of the newest tank battalion of the SS. As the boys approached the vicinity where Adolf Hitler was to review the passing of the troops, they marveled at the giant swastika flags which were draped from the top of massive columns which lined the length of the avenue.

On the very top of the columns were huge flat bowls and Karl remembered faintly that before the war, the bowls were filled with oil and set afire. Not every day of course, but he remembered seeing the columns ablaze like giant torches, especially in 1936 during the Olympic Games.

Now, it seemed that all the city workers were tasked to conceal the wide avenue from observation from above. Huge nettings with artificial shrubs spanned from column to column and across the streets in this particular area of the city.

"Do you think that we will be close enough to hear the speech of our Fuehrer?" asked Harold as he watched a team of radio technicians setting up a row of microphones in the center of the grandstand. Karl looked around before he answered and then pointed at the huge drums of cables being unrolled along "Unter den Linden" the main thoroughfare through the park.

"These could be cables of a public address system. Let's see if we can locate the loudspeakers." A short time later the boys witnessed the installation of dozens and dozens of loudspeakers all throughout the park and up and down the main avenue.

Judging by all the preparations, it promised to be a spectacular event.

ELEVEN

The boys had decided to visit grandpa Veth early in the day because their Jungvolk practice started in the afternoon.

"Ever seen something like that?" he asked the boys as he handed each one an almost identical piece of paper. It was a regular sheet of writing paper with small numbers all over the place.

"No," said Karl. He looked at it from all sides because he could not decipher what it could be. Since he was very fast in arithmetic, he added the figures in his head and then divided the summation of the left side of the paper with the summation of the right side, but the result made no sense to him.

"Please explain, Herr Veth," said Harold, turning the paper upside down. "We have training and practice duty this afternoon. I could stand here all day and I would still not know what it means."

"I hoped that you did not know what it was. It is a very simple game and called connect the numbers."

He handed each of the boys a colored pencil. "Now start at the lowest number you can find and connect to the next number and keep on connecting until you reach the last number. Go ahead, do it now. It only takes a few minutes and then you can go on your way."

Karl had already detected that the lowest number on his paper was 15 and by the time his grandpa finished the instructions he was busy connecting. In nothing flat, the boys looked at a modest picture.

Harold was holding a picture of a dragon in his hand. Karl had drawn a galloping horse.

"I know that this is a simple children's game, but the object of today's lesson is to show you how simple it is to make sense of a mumble jumble from seemingly random figures, or events if you will, by simply connecting the dots." The old man explained.

"That's it?" wondered Karl. "For today's lesson you had us draw a couple of animals?" He still did not get the full meaning. To his surprise Harold was clearly ahead of him because he thanked the grandpa for the excellent lesson.

"Connect the events, your grandpa said. We need to connect the unfolding events in order to get an understanding of the whole picture. What's the matter with you, slow poke?" Harold enjoyed that he was outthinking his friend. Usually it was the other way around.

"I am not done. Do you have another ten minutes?" asked the grandfather as he placed another piece of paper on the table.

"Sure," said Karl as he tried to steal a look at the new diagram. Both boys were keen to receive the remainder of the lesson.

"Just look at it this one and then look at these ones," said the cavalry officer as he placed two more papers on the table. Karl was the first to recognize that the two additional papers were merely duplicates of the numbered papers they had just completed. However, the third single paper was a puzzle for sure.

There were little circles and hooks, dots and seemingly random numbers. Some of the numbers were even upside down or sideways. He tried to look for the lowest number and the second lowest but all he could discern was a low upside down single digit number 4 and the next highest number was a 14. To make it even more confusing, these two numbers were right next to each other. There was no obvious reason to connect them.

Harold shrugged his shoulders and laid his picture of the dragon next to the likewise numbered picture. "These two belong together, and so does Karl's two papers. But the third one has nothing to do with the other ones."

"What is your take on these depictions?" the old warrior asked his grandson.

"I am with Harold that this one has no relationship with the other ones." He pointed at the picture with the hooks and circles, holding on to his drawing and the likewise numbered paper.

"What makes you believe that the two pictures in your hand are connected?" His grandpa asked, pronouncing the word 'believe".

Karl's face lit up. "I understand what you are trying to say, Grandpa. I don't need to 'believe' that these two belong together because I 'know' that they are the same. I recognize the numbers and the patterns."

"Very well, then what about the third one? Other from the fact that it is not connected to either one of your previously drawn images?"

Karl turned to his friend. "What do you make of it?"

"Nothing. There is obviously a lot more information on this diagram. But I don't know what to do with it," his friend assured him.

Both boys looked at the grandfather for some explanation.

"Take the picture along and figure it out while you are thinking about it. I'll give you a hint. Use your mind." He looked at his grandson and Harold. Both boys were wearing their uniforms as they wanted to go from him to the Jungvolk office. He noted a red and white small rope on Karl's shirt. It was leading from the button of the breast pocket to a higher button on the center of the shirt.

"What is this rope you are wearing? I don't see it on Harold's shirt," he asked.

"This identifies me as an Oberjungschaftsfuehrer, it's the second lowest designation of a leader in the Jungvolk. I earned this promotion last week for completing my six-month stint as a sub leader in the KLV camp."

Karl's grandfather nodded his approval. "Yes, I heard from your father that your elementary schooling is coming to an end. Congratulations on your test results. I am proud of you." He shook hands with both of the boys as they left the apartment.

"I could see that I was drawing a horse before I finished the picture," Karl remarked on their way to the meeting place.

"I guess you could," said Harold, "but I could not. I have never seen a dragon, except in some drawings of Siegfried in his fights with a dragon in the Teutoburger Woods."

"You are right," said Karl, "as often as we went to a zoo, I never saw a dragon either."

"You know why? Don't you?" Harold had a disgusted expression in his face. "Fire spitting dragons are inventions of a very sick mind," he proclaimed.

Karl was not so eager to agree with his friend. "Come on, Harold. We have both seen the little lizards and salamanders. They are just miniature dragons. It could very well be that in ancient times they were a lot larger."

"Maybe so and maybe not," allowed Harold. "However, they never spit fire. This depiction alone is sick, sick, sick." He was almost spitting the words.

"Now, now, Harold, what you consider sick, some other people may declare artistic. Remember, even Herr Halama told us that artists may enjoy from time to time a certain freedom in expressing themselves."

Harold stopped in his tracks and looked at Karl in disgust. "If you were not my friend I would no longer talk to you. But, I have to tell you that I don't understand you. There was an SS speaker in our school who warned us of people like you. He described it as a liberal attitude and told us that in time the Nazi system will get rid of all liberal elements. If I were you I would keep my mouth shut."

He started walking again and Karl ambled to keep up with him. He did not like the direction their discussion was going.

"You know what, Harold? We are ambitious to learn as much as we can because we both know that we are just beginning to understand the adult world. I think in our dialogue there is a lesson for both of us." He almost had to run to keep up with the long steps of his taller friend.

Harold slowed down a bit and looked at him. "Tell me the lesson, Karl. But please without any liberal garbage, if you can."

"I can do that in one sentence. Provided that you slow down enough so I can talk to you face-to-face."

Harold stopped and locked eyes with Karl. "Go ahead, tell me."

Karl did not blink. "We should not criticize or put things down we don't understand," he said firmly and then added, "I for one don't even know what liberal means and I doubt that you do. But at the very least we should agree to keep an open mind."

Harold laughed. "Agreed. If all people could talk to each other like we just did and then agree to keep an open mind," he interrupted himself to think, "I think it would be beneficial to all of us."

"There you go, Harold, I agree with you too, but what is beneficial?"

Harold was still laughing. "Your granddad is right. You can't speak three sentences without asking a question. But, earnestly, Karl, you should also learn to keep your mouth shut."

Karl was taking his friend's advice seriously but he could not help thinking that if he should be careful in saying what was on his mind, then his grandpa should really watch out.

***

When the boys arrived at the assembly point they were surprised to see some trucks waiting to transport them to the venue in the Tiergarten.

There were literally thousands of members of the HJ and the

Jungvolk lined up as far as the eye could see. The boy's unit was called 4/6/1/37.

The number 4 stood for Jungzug 4 (a unit of about 60 boys).

The number 6 stood for Faehnlein 6 (a larger unit of about 180 boys)

The number 1 stood for Stamm 1 (a unit of about 1000 boys).

The number 37 stood for Bann 37 (a specific area of Berlin).

Karl's particular unit was ordered to stand directly across from Hitler's grandstand. To Karl's enjoyment, this was the first time that his small size was of an advantage. Their 'Stamm' was ordered to stand six lines deep alongside the avenue. Because of his short stature Karl was standing in the very front row. He was facing the grandstand a little bit left off the center. The boys were instructed to stand close to each other and on the command of 'Koppelschluss' they had to grip into the side of the belt of the boys standing next to them. Since everyone did this they were forming a human chain six rows deep. The next command was 'Zwischenman," meaning that the boys were not supposed to stand directly behind each other but were facing the small vacant spot between the boys standing in front of them.

It was a fairly simple and extremely fast exercise. It was repeated over and over until everyone understood the commands.

Two days later, on the day of the event, a Saturday, the boys had to assemble at their office at 6 AM. The trucks were again waiting and when their unit 4/6/1/37 was dropped off in the Tiergarten, the boys were overwhelmed to see the masses of people. In spite of the early morning hour, there were thousands waiting to get a glimpse of their beloved Fuehrer, Adolf Hitler. They were kept inbound and away from the street by huge trucks which were lined bumper to bumper on the avenue. Karl's unit was getting into formation, six boys deep, about a mile away from the grandstand and started to march. In front of their Jungvolk Stamm was a unit of 200 HJ drummers and in front of them were 50 HJ flag carriers.

When they were about half a mile away from the grandstand, orders penetrated the early morning air and the unit broke into running double time. The drummers started a staccato of high speed drumming, the flags got curled halfway around the mast and the carriers lowered them into a slanted position, pointing forward.

The Stamm #1/37 was the role model for all the HJ formations in Berlin and their exact and disciplined storm commando of the combined HJ and Jungvolk was indeed a sight to behold.

The unit stormed down the avenue and stopped when it reached the area by the grandstand. The crowd behind the trucks roared their approval and Karl was so proud of himself that tears came to his eyes.

While the drummers slowed down to a precise beat, the flag-carrying unit marched across the avenue and took up positions besides the stand. Karl's unit stopped exactly at the same spot they had trained on two days ago. Upon the command 'left turn' Karl stood again in the first line. "Koppelschluss," came the next order and Karl gripped the belts of the boys on his right and on his left and the boys in return got a hold of his belt. "Zwischenman," yelled the Stamm leader and while Karl and his comrades on his right and left did not move, the boys behind him stepped half a step to the sides.

As soon as they stood still the trucks began to move out and the mass of people who had waited behind the trucks moved like a wave towards the human barrier of the boys. Everyone wanted to be close to the road. In spite of the fact that the cordon was six boys deep it swayed back and forth until the pressure of the mob subsided. The Jungvolk did their assigned job and was holding the avenue free of the waiting masses. A short time later the boys were ordered to stand at ease and they were also allowed to talk to each other.

It was 9:00 AM and the parade of the panzers was planned for 4:00 PM. Adolf Hitler was scheduled to speak at 6:00 PM and the crowd of thousands was waiting. The ones in front of the multitude had been here since the past night.

"I doubt that we will be able to keep the mob away from the street when our Fuehrer arrives," the boy on the right of Karl opinioned.

"Maybe we will receive reinforcement," Karl speculated.

"There never have been any reinforcements." answered the boy. "My name is Herbert. You must be a newcomer. I have never seen you in barrier duty." Herbert extended his hand to Karl. He was of about equal height with Karl and seemed to be of the same age.

"I have been in a KLV camp during the last few months. My name is Karl Veth," Karl introduced himself. "Have you ever seen the Fuehrer up close?" he inquired.

"Yes," answered Herbert, "sometimes he was within a few feet of me. How about you?"

"No, never that close. But I have seen him very often. Mostly on his birthday on the balcony of the Reich Chancellery."

"Yes," answered Herbert, "I have seen him there too." He looked at the rope dangling on Karl's shirt. "How did you receive your promotions? You are the youngest Oberjungschaftsfuehrer I have ever met."

"They were routine promotions due to my position as a sub leader of a KLV camp." Karl answered truthfully. Herbert recoiled for a second.

"I know about you. Karl Veth, right? You are the guy who introduced kitchen duty in the camps." He shook Karl's hand again. "Everybody is talking about you. Let me know when you join another camp. I'd like to go with you."

Karl could not help himself and smiled. "Why? You like to peel potatoes?"

"Not really," laughed Herbert. "We heard that you always managed to reward the work units. I would not mind cleaning toilets or bathrooms as long as I don't have to attend school hours."

Karl joined his laugh. "Thanks for the ideas, Herbert. If you have excellent grades I might be able to arrange for you a position as a sub leader."

"Excellent grades? No Karl, you are confusing me with someone who is ambitious. I like to avoid school because I hate it."

Karl had to think what Harold had told him about choosing the correct words to communicate. This Herbert seemed to be a likable fellow, except that he had used the word 'hate' to describe his distaste for the school. Karl did not like the word. It was too extreme for his taste. He liked to use the time he was wasting by standing around and decided to experiment with some words.

"Hate?" He repeated to make sure that there was no misunderstanding. "Now this is a rather strong word. I venture that you strongly dislike schools, or is it the new female teachers which you don't like?"

Herbert looked for a second as if he did not understand the question. Then it dawned on him and he smiled once more at Karl. "Come on Karl, I am sure that you won't report what I am saying. You heard me alright. I hate learning and I hate school, I hate it, I hate it, I hate it."

Karl got the drift. Herbert hated school. So much for the experiment. "Alright, I get it. Then I take it that you like sports?" Karl wanted to keep the conversation going when he heard the boy on his left.

"I also hate the school," the boy said.

Nice going Karl, he thought to himself. "What about soccer?" he prompted both boys and just as he expected, the mood instantly changed.

"Yeah, soccer," exclaimed Herbert. "That's where it's at. I can manipulate the ball up and down the court. Once I have control of him nobody is able to take him away from me." Herbert was obviously proud of himself.

The boy on Karl's left was not to be outdone. "Yes, Herbert is good at it, but so am I. And I love the cheering of the classmates when we score a goal. You don't get this kind of cheering when you recite the multiplication tables or spell a word correctly," he informed Karl, who admitted that the boys were right on this point. He looked at the boy on his left and stuck out his hand. "I am Karl Veth."

"Yes, I overheard your conversation." He gave Karl's hand a firm shake. "My name is also Herbert."

Karl did not blink. "I take it that you two are brothers."

TWELVE

Karl enjoyed the stupid look he received from the boys. He was just about to start the conversation again when the order for Koppelschluss prompted the boys to firm up. He reached for the belts of the Herberts, determined not to let go.

He looked down the length of the boulevard where a group of Wehrmacht (army) motorcyclists came up. They were followed by several black Mercedes limousines which carried officers of the Wehrmacht and the SS.

All of them stopped for a moment between the HJ cordon and the grandstand to unload the military bigwigs. As each of the officers reached their designated seat, the loudspeakers announced their rank followed by their name.

Karl could clearly see Franz Halder from the General Staff and Wilhelm Keitel, the chief commander of the Wehrmacht. This was also the first time that he saw Admiral E. Raeder, Chief of the German Navy. The loudspeaker announced many names he did not recognize and he was surprised that apparently none of the well-known Panzer officers were present.

The dignitaries were barely seated when another motorcycle brigade announced the final two limousines. The first one stopped again in the same place and Karl heard that the dignitary was none other than the Chief of the German Intelligence Service, W.F. Canaris. He was accompanied by Dr. Josef Goebbels, the propaganda Minister of Germany.

The last car was a black Mercedes convertible. It carried Adolf Hitler and stopped about fifty feet short of the grandstand. As usual on these occasions, Herr Hitler got out and walked over to the cordon of the Jungvolk and started to shake hands with some of the boys. As he slowly walked towards Karl's position the pressure of the throng of people behind the human barrier became nearly too much to bear.

The crowd roared constantly their *hail, hail, hail* and pushed forward to get a better look at their beloved Fuehrer.

Karl noted that Herr Hitler walked alone; no body guards or secret service agents were needed to protect him because the population loved him. Karl counted that the Fuehrer shook hands with every fifth or so boy from the barrier detail. He started to figure in his head what the chances were that the Fuehrer would shake hands with him or at least lock eyes with him. But about 15 feet from Karl the Fuehrer turned away from the cordon and crossed the street towards his place on the grandstand.

Karl was more than disappointed but his mood changed when the first Panzerjaeger (panzer hunter) vehicles rolled slowly by. They were followed by all terrain troop carriers and the only difference seemed to be the thickness of the armor protecting the wheels.

The most impressive thing was the exact distance the vehicles kept between each other. It was as if they were all connected by invisible steel rods. After they passed, the air started to fill with the deep roar of the approaching heavy Tiger I engines.

The 101st SS Tiger I Panzer Battalion was grinding slowly but steadily toward them. The tank commanders in their black double-breasted jackets were standing straight in the turret. Their faces were turned towards the stand and their fingertips seemed to be glued to their black berets until they were directly opposite from the Fuehrer. Only then did they stretch their arm to the Nazi salute.

Thirty-six rows of panzers, six deep, made the asphalt reverberate and Karl thought that he could actually feel the power and mighty force projected by the parade. It was planned to be an impressive sight and it was. Karl was sure that any one of the spectators would remember this afternoon for the rest of his or her life.

In all this excitement it was no wonder that Karl had somehow missed the arrival of the military band. Maybe they had assembled or arrived when he was still talking with the boys. But now they were impossible to miss. To Karl's astonishment they were accompanied by the fanfares from his 4/6/1/37 unit. As they played the national anthem, the last unit of motorcycles passed by.

The parade was over and Hitler started to address the crowd. The public communication system worked flawlessly and Hitler's voice could be heard in the last corner of the Tiergarten.

Hitler's address was constantly interrupted by the thundering cheer of the crowd. After Hitler stopped, Karl could not remember what the speech was about. But he would never forget the intensity delivered by one of the greatest orators the world had ever seen.

"Man," exclaimed Harold several hours later on their way home, "Hitler does not hesitate to call his enemies by name and when he does, he leaves no doubt of what he thinks about them or what he means."

"Yes," agreed Karl, "and when he asked for help and sacrifices of the 'civilians' you felt compelled to comply."

"And, did you feel the excitement of the masses? How can it be that thousands of people love him and are prepared to die for him, when other intelligent people, like your grandpa despise him?" Harold was not so much asking his friend as he was wondering aloud about the event they had witnessed.

Karl was still agitated when he arrived home and told his parents about his impressions. His father was more interested in the details of the Tiger Panzers than in Hitler's personality and he mentioned that he would not cross the street to see him up close. His mother, on the other hand wanted to know everything about him.

"Was he really impressive?" she asked of Karl.

"I don't know what you mean by impressive, Mutti. He is not very tall, not like grandpa. But he walked with energy and confidence, if that is what you want to know."

"What about his eyes? I know that they are dark. But, are they hard as some people claim or are they warm?"

Karl did not have to think because he had also wanted to see the eyes of the Fuehrer. "I am sorry Mutti, Herr Hitler walked away from where I was standing. I never saw his eyes".

His mother looked toward the picture of Hitler hanging on the wall. "I think we need a leader like this man," she said.

Karl's father said nothing. He did not even like the picture, but in 1942 every German family had a picture of the Fuehrer displayed in their home. When Karl's mother bought it, it stood for weeks in a corner of the hallway until his father found the time to hang it up. Karl could feel some tension between his parents whenever the conversation shifted towards politics. Since there was nothing he could do about it, he always started to play with his brother and his little sister until his parents' conversation drifted to other subjects.

The next day there was a letter from the KLV administration announcing that the mandatory evacuation of school children was imminent. The administration strongly encouraged the parents to send their children to relatives in the country before the evacuation regulations would take effect. Karl remembered that just a few days ago his former school principal had been arrested by the SS when he made the 'inflammatory' remark that the schools in Berlin were soon to be evacuated.

He could not help recognizing that the SS and the Gestapo were the overriding authority. He wondered how this would affect his upcoming position as a sub leader in the KLV camps and decided not to invent or install any new programs.

He had always looked to his father and grandfather for guidance and to the school teachers as role models. Was he now to look at the SS or to the Gestapo for shining examples? He thought of principal Groneberg from Usedom as a nice stand-out teacher.

There was no doubt that the Gestapo who arrested principal Groneberg was the agency in power and in charge, but he could not equate them as being equal to the man they had arrested. And still his friend Harold had told him that the Nazis with their newly installed authorities like the Secret State Police were in essence, the constructors of the new 1,000-year Reich.

***

"Grandpa, I am confused and need your advice," he asked when he went with Harold to see the old cavalry officer.

"Don't think that you are the only one who is confused. You are only 12 years old and I know many adults who don't know what time it is. Exactly now, Karl, what kind of advice do you need?"

Karl deliberated how he could frame his question and then decided on the direct approach.

"Opa, the SS arrested my school principal and I am supposed to visit various KLV camps and write essays about their conditions for the HJ periodicals. I am also to write reports to the KLV authorities. Should I submit all my essays and reports to the SS or to the Secret State Police for their approval? I mean, before I send them to the KLV authorities or the HJ? What would you do?"

"This is hard to answer, Karl. When I was your age we knew who was in charge and acted accordingly. Now it seems that there are conflicting agendas even within our armed forces." The old man reached for a newspaper, looking at a story describing the retreat of the German army in Russia.

"Here, read this. It is very evident that the SS is competing with the Wehrmacht. Except that the SS has the backing of Adolf Hitler. All evidence points towards Herr Hitler wanting to restrain the officer corps of the Army. He condemned the action of General Paulus who was surrendering in Stalingrad after he lost more than 90 % of his men. If I were a military reporter, I would cover my behind and run my writings by the SS for approval."

He looked at Karl who did not even glimpse at the newspaper. He read all about the retreats of the German forces. He would have liked a more direct answer to his predicament.

"So, are you saying that I should send my reports to the SS for approval?"

"No, Karl. If I were you, I would send all the essays and reports to the HJ headquarters in Berlin, with the request to forward them to the pertinent offices. Finish. You did what you were tasked to do and shifted the responsibility to the HJ which is the 'darling' of Herr Hitler anyway."

Karl like the answer from his grandpa. It seemed to be very good advice and very easy to follow.

Harold placed the sheet of paper with all the numbers and dots in front of grandpa. "Sorry, Herr Veth. We are giving up. I have only a few days left in Berlin and we would like to know what this means."

Karl nodded his agreement.

"This is essentially the same as the other ones." The grandfather pulled a pencil out of the kitchen drawer and began connecting numbers which followed each other. He ignored all the hooks and dots and other symbols. Some of his connecting lines were only between two numbers and others were connecting several numbers.

When he was done the boys saw to their astonishment the perfect image of a peacock. All of the hooks were part of feathers and the little circles and dots were part of the plume. The upside down and sideway numbers were not really numbers anymore but part of the beak and eyes. In all reality, there were just a few numbers which had been upside down but they had been enough of a diversion to mislead the onlooker.

"It is not as complicated as you think," said Karl's grandpa, "You will hardly ever see through a mess of information. What you need to do, to get a true picture of what you are looking at, you need to connect the dots. In this case you needed to connect the numbers which you recognized as being related. The remainder will more or less fall into place as the picture evolves."

He went back into the kitchen and looked at the clock over the oven. "If you have the time I would like to show you something. We need about two hours." The boys had the time and were happy to go with him. Their destination was the Funkturm, the radio tower and highest tower in Berlin in 1942.

This time the grandpa used the street cars to get there because there was no direct subway connection. Karl knew the area. The Funkturm was close to the Olympic Stadium.

In 1936, when he was 6 years old, his father had taken him to see some of the Olympic events. He still remembered the huge searchlights. The beams from the lights had formed an illuminated tent over the stadium under which, spectacular fireworks closed out the games on the final night.

The grandfather led the way to the Funkturm and stopped when he came to the base of the steel-frame work construction. Harold and Karl hoped that they would enter the high-speed elevator to visit the observation deck, but the cavalry officer had something different in mind. He pointed to one of the park benches surrounding the area.

"Let's sit down," he invited the boys. "I showed you how switches are set in advance. This here, today, is a similar lesson."

He leaned against the back board of the bench and looked up to the big restaurant which surrounded the steel structure at the height of 170 feet. "This tower was started in 1924 and it was completed in 1926. It is 452 feet tall. In order to build such a structure you have to follow well laid out plans."

With his shoes he pushed together a small mound of sand. "Look at this. If I were to tell you that this tiny knoll is the complete foundation for a tower you would know that it would hardly support more than a little twig." He picked up a small stick and pushed it in the center of the small heap of dirt where it promptly toppled over. "See, it does not even support the little branch." He looked to find an even smaller stick to plant in the sand.

"Now let's look at foundation of the Funkturm." He got up and walked to the concrete boulders of the base. He stepped up the distance between the outside edges. "You can see that they are 65 feet apart."

He returned to the bench. "I don't know how many tons of concrete it took to cement the outer steel girders in place but even without that information, and without knowing the plans, I would have known just by looking at the distance between the anchor points that this was the foundation of a giant structure."

The old man looked intently at the boys. "Do you understand what I am saying? You cannot build any kind of a structure without building first an adequate foundation."

"Yes, Opa, I think that what you are telling us is somehow related to setting switches and to connecting dots." Karl ventured.

"Exactly," smiled the grandfather. "Our lessons started when you were asking me why we are having a war. I decided to broaden the lessons so you can anticipate and prepare for the various events you will encounter during your lifetime."

"If I understand you correctly, Herr Veth, you are telling us that we should watch out for events and how they relate to each other by connecting the dots." Harold was eager to participate.

"Yes," confirmed the old man. "This will give you a chance to see or to understand the whole picture and by looking at the size of a foundation you are able to estimate the size of the planned structure."

He got up and started to lead the way home because he wanted the boys to digest what he had told them. He wanted them to think for themselves.

Karl's next question confirmed that the boys were thinking.

"Opa, I try to understand but I am not clear how the lesson with the switches relate to what you taught us today."

The grandfather turned and sat down again. "Karl, setting the switches in advance is a metaphor for many things. In answer to your very first question regarding the reason for the present war, I explained that the switches for this event had been set before Herr Hitler came to power. He did not set the switches himself. They were already solid in place."

He tried to find a soft spot on the hard bench, shifted around, and finally gave up.

"Are they always set by events or are they also set by people?" Harold followed up.

"The answer is both. Many events are caused by people and because people die and fade away, it is difficult to later on detect accurately the precise cause. Many other events are caused by nature but it is again how people react to an event of nature which sets the switches down the road."

The old man stretched and got up again. "Look, we can elaborate on this forever. The important thing is that we recognize what is going on around us. If we recognize it in time and if it bothers us, we might be able to do something about it," he stretched some more. "If we wish," he added.

"What if we are unable to do anything about it, not because we are unwilling, but simply because we are too small or too weak?" Karl wanted to know.

The grandfather started to walk back to the street car station. "You mean as in the eruption of a volcano? Well, first of all, you should not build your home too close to a known upheaval. Second, if you did, and the mountain begins to belch, then you need to run away. Third, if it is too late to run away, you need to take cover."

He walked a step faster to catch the next street car.

"This is the very reason I told you to connect the dots. Even a volcano rumbles before it spits fire."

THIRTEEN

A few days later, Harold received the good news that he was accepted into the language program. There were two Napola schools with a special program for languages and he was sent to Potsdam. It was not directly in the city of Potsdam but in a campus on the outskirts.

The boys had spent the days before his departure together by exploring different subway destinations. One of these excursions led them to Dahlem, in the Zehlendorf district.

In the 'old Berlin' before 1936, it was a suburb of Berlin. Now, however, in 1942, the city of Berlin was called 'Grossberlin" meaning "Great Berlin" and most, if not all, of the outlying areas had been incorporated into the city.

"Can you believe all these wonderful private homes?" marveled Karl. It was the first time that he was in a part of Berlin without apartment houses.

"This is like a dream," agreed Harold. "I wonder who is able to afford to live in homes like these."

Karl considered his friend's question for a few seconds. "You know, Harold. This is something our elders miss in all their teachings."

"What do you mean?"

"I mean they should take us to these nice places and then tell us what it is that these people do for a living. And then they should take us to the poorest neighborhoods in Berlin and say something like *'this is where you will have to live if you don't get ambitious and improve your grades."*

"Yes," agreed Harol. He stopped to read the name plate of the house owner. "Dr. Ferdinand Bluecher, there you have it. But they cannot all be doctors."

"That's exactly what I am thinking, Harold. If the adults would show us what our grades in school are able to accomplish in life we would have far fewer slackers. I am happy that we made this little trip. But I will ask my father or my grandfather about these people who live here."

They walked for a few blocks and then turned around to take the subway home.

"You want to visit Moabit?" asked Harold. "I heard that it is one of the poorest neighborhoods."

"Are you out of your mind?" Karl shuddered. "I don't need to see misery to enjoy myself. Now, if you say 'Wannsee' then I am all for it." Wannsee was a small lakeside community and could be reached with the S bahn, the city train.

The boys took the subway to Gleisdreieck, the major station where the grandfather had taken the boys before. There they changed to a city train to visit the small resort-like suburb. Again, it was like Harold had said before; they walked like in a dream as they gaped at the lakeside homes.

"Cannot be all doctors," said Harold again as they boarded the train back.

"No," agreed Karl, "I wonder if even a teacher could afford to live here. I will surely ask my dad about it."

"Teachers are so smart, I am sure that they can live anyplace they wish," opinionated Harold.

"I think you might be wrong, Harold. Teachers are not that smart. All they do is read something to us and then conduct tests. I think that my Opa is a better teacher than any we had in school."

"Could be, but your grandpa was an officer. I think that officers have to be smart to be officers."

"I still think that you are wrong, Harold, at least as far as the teachers are concerned. Look, I passed the final elementary school graduation tests without any teachers. I am two years ahead of our class just by reading and studying."

"Alright, Karl, maybe teachers don't live in the homes we just visited," allowed Harold, "but I sure would like to know who does. I will ask my father too."

***

When Karl got home he was prepared for a meager supper because it was a two meal day. He was pleasantly surprised when his mother served the family a large dish of potato soup.

"Herr Hitler increased our rations," his mother informed him,

"Pappa told me that we are able to have three meals a day again."

Karl looked at his father who shook his head. "No, Mutti, Herr Hitler has nothing to do with this. It is a change in the administration of the rationing office that is responsible. The new administrator is more capable than the previous one. I doubt very much that Herr Hitler even understands anything about rationing or food reserve management."

Karl's mother was undeterred. "Then it must have been our Fuehrer who initiated the change in the administration," she maintained. "He is in charge of everything."

Karl got up and looked for some toy to play with his brother. He loved his mother with all his heart but he did not understand why his parents disagreed on anything that Hitler said or did.

It was shortly before 8:00 PM and Karl looked over to the radio hoping that his father would turn it on. It was Saturday evening and there was always some music program after the news.

However, his father never allowed anyone to touch the radio. He had bought it two years ago and it was his prerogative to decide when the family was entitled to hear anything else but the news.

The news was broadcasted every evening at 8:00 PM and every evening at that time his father would turn on the radio. He insisted that all the lights had to be turned off when the radio was turned on and nobody was allowed to talk.

Then the whole family, including his little brother, would huddle in front of the receiver and listen to the OKW - or military headquarters - report. The report lasted maybe 15 minutes and then his father turned the radio off and turned the lights back on.

Only on Saturday evening and on Sunday afternoon at 2:00 PM did his father allow the family to listen to one hour of music.

The news this evening was just as hopeless as on the previous day. The German lines were retreating and Dr. Goebbels, the head of the propaganda agency, promised that the wonder weapons were nearing completion and once employed would shred the enemy.

Karl's father changed the station to the only one broadcasting music. Tonight's feature was some light opera music and while his parents listened, Karl started to repack some suitcases. The suitcase for his upcoming trip was already packed but there were three other ones that were designated air raid shelter cases. His father insisted that the suitcases should provide food for three days.

"If the four-story building collapses and blocks the exits we might have to wait several days until someone digs us out." The family had decided on water, milk powder and some cans of margarine and liverwurst. In addition, every week or so, they replaced the dried bread. It was called Knaeckebrot and was similar to Rye Crisp. It was a little bit salty but otherwise it served its purpose.

The packing proved to be a little bit complicated because the air wardens had gas masks distributed which were now a required necessity to pack. The large masks for Karl and his parents had individual round canisters and could be slung over the shoulder. However, the smaller one for his brother was bulky and cumbersome to pack. The real small one was a monstrosity compared to his 2-year-old sister's head. It looked not only grotesque on her, but it was also ill-fitting. Karl doubted that it would even do its job.

"Will you please look at this," he implored his mother who had thought that she fitted the mask somehow wrongly during the gas exercises. "This cannot possibly prevent the gas from reaching her face," Karl said again and pointed to the wide airspace between the mask and his sister's face.

His parents did not have an answer. There were supposedly some smaller gasmasks but the local warden was unable to supply any.

"I will ask Harold," Karl announced. "His father is in charge of some kind of warehouses. Maybe he knows how to get a real small mask." He stuffed the mask in a paper bag to give to Harold. Hopefully he could exchange it.

Karl was done with the packing and listened with his parents for a few more minutes to the radio before his father declared: "No more music for today." He turned the radio off and placed a small tablecloth over it so it would not get dusty.

***

"I have a gasmask which is too large for my sister. You mentioned your father's position. You think he might be able to help us out?" Karl asked his friend on the next day.

"You know, Karl, my father never really told me what warehouses he is in charge off. But I know that he is able to get us most anything. I think that he trades a lot." Harold looked at the gasmask. "Are you telling me that there are smaller versions? This one looks very tiny already".

Karl shrugged his shoulders. "I only know that this one here does not fit my sister. Can you please ask your dad about it?"

"I will," said Harold and while he took the paper bag he handed Karl a sandwich with Brotaufstrich, a type of bread spread. It was a new product that was supposed to replace butter or margarine. It was greasy and had no real taste of its own. Whoever manufactured it must have been under the illusion that the consumer would spread it on the bread and then add some other item on top of it, like cheese or liverwurst. However, none of these other items were available. The people who lived in the country gathered some herb-like nettles which they dried and sprinkled on top of the spread. The people in the cities just sprinkled some salt on it. The salt somehow made the greasy taste more pleasant.

"Thank you," said Karl. He had no salt or nettles. He was happy to have something extra to eat.

It was Sunday afternoon and the boys were on their way to the Jungvolk meeting place. The first thing they noted was the absence of all their older leaders. There was only an SS officer who told them that all the HJ members over 16 years of age were being drafted into labor details.

"What kind of labor?" asked Karl.

"Digging ditches and building shelters outside of Berlin."

"What kind of shelters are they building?" asked Harold.

The officer told him to mind his own business and to go home. They would be notified of their new assembly places within a week.

"Rudy was a nice guy. I wonder if we will see him again." Harold was worried because just a few days ago he had heard his father say that all the boys 16 years and older were being drafted to serve in the infantry. The boys had dismissed it as a rumor, because every other day there was another disturbing news story and so far their older HJ members had still been around.

Karl suggested spending the remainder of the afternoon in the subway. He had found some time ago an underground walkway which he had never seen before. It was kind of crude and not as well constructed as the regular walkways. At first he had speculated that it was a short-cut for maintenance workers but when he followed it to the end, it did not seem to connect to anything and he wanted to show it to his friend before they parted on their individual missions.

"See, Harold. This is just a blind tunnel. It is not leading anywhere." Karl carried a small flashlight and the battery was near the end of its life.

"Direct the light to the floor on the end," suggested Harold.

Karl let the meager light dance around the floor and saw what Harold was pointing out. At the very end of the tunnel was a culvert leading slightly down. It was blocked with a large grate, which looked like it was anchored in concrete.

"This could be a drain pipe in case the subway gets flooded in a major storm. I wonder where it leads to." Harold speculated as he tried to unhook the grate from its locks. The culvert looked large enough to allow a person to crawl through it.

"No, I don't think so," said Karl.

"Why not?" challenged Harold.

"Well, for one thing, this passageway is not descending. It almost felt as if we were going a little bit uphill. For another, this foot path looks like it is being used. Look at all the foot prints in the dust." He directed his light down again but the battery gave finally out. The boys were in complete darkness. "I am sure that I saw several foot prints," he repeated, "I should have looked at the floor when I was here the first time. Let's go back and come back tomorrow with new batteries."

Karl took the lead back and after the first turn they could see the first maintenance lights of the regular subway system ahead of them.

"Maybe it is an entryway to a building. Maybe a fire station or something like that." Harold guessed.

"Could be, as far as a special purpose building, but why a culvert with a grate blocking it?" Karl could not think of an answer. They exited the subway system through an airshaft close to the zoo station.

"We could come back with a compass and measure the distance and the direction. This way we might be able to ascertain what kind of building is above the shaft." Harold suggested. "But why do we want to know?"

Karl shrugged his shoulders. "I really would like to know because the entry from the regular subway tunnel is almost hidden. I only found it by accident when I stumbled over a small pile of dirt. It is not a passage way for the subway workers. That much is sure."

"Do you think that it matters to us what this is about?" Harold wanted to be supportive but was also ready to drop the subject.

"I don't think that it matters to us, but we know almost all of the system and that we do not know the purpose of this path bothers me."

"Alright, then it's settled. We will come back with a compass." Harold agreed. "We only have one more day and then I have to report to the campus by Potsdam."

***

All evening long Karl was thinking about the possible purpose of the tunnel and he was wondering to himself why he was unable to dismiss it from his mind. *I will think about it real hard before I fall asleep,* he decided. It was a technique his father had told him to employ whenever he was searching for an answer. Sometimes it worked but most of the time it did not produce anything but a headache.

Karl decided to ask his dad if he was missing something with the technique or how he could do it better.

"How often did it work in relationship to your efforts to find an answer?" His father asked.

"Not very often."

"Well then, we know that it sometimes works. Just train yourself by asking yourself easy questions. The more answers you get, the more efficient you will become in producing answers to the more important questions." Herr Veth spoke to his son in a very assertive tone as if there was no doubt in his mind.

Karl thanked his father and wished his parents good night when his father called him back. "I forgot to ask you, do you expect the answers in the morning when you awake, or did you notice that they sometimes pop up in the middle of the week, or when you expect them the least?"

Karl had to think. "Maybe it was more often that I found the answers a few days later. How long do you wait, Pappa?"

Herr Veth wanted to be sure that Karl understood correctly and he spoke slowly.

"I just wait. In the meantime I simply open myself up to observe what is around me. Because the answer is always all around us."

Karl had no reason to doubt his father. He just wanted some more detailed instructions. "Is there any procedure I have to do to train myself?"

"No, no special procedure. Just let yourself drift off to sleep while you gently think about your questions."

"I would like to believe you, Pappa, but if it is this simple, why don't the military leaders employ this method and win all the battles?"

"Karl, you are thinking in the wrong direction. Don't think about why things don't work. We will take this up again when you are older or ready for it. In the meantime, it is important that you just allow yourself to think that it is possible.

Karl's father got up and took an encyclopedia from his book cabinet. He wanted to look up some famous names.

"Did your teachers ever tell you that many inventors have more than one patent in their lifetime of achievements?"

"Yes, of course. Thomas Edison was one I learned about. He had over 1,000 patents to his name."

"Alright, and have you also heard about very smart people who do not hold a single patent?"

"Yes, I have, Friedrich Nietzsche is one of them."

"Good, now just consider for a moment that maybe there was no difference between them. Edison thought about a technical problem and then started to believe that he could solve it. He allowed himself to believe in himself. He also allowed himself to believe that he could invent more than just one single thing. Eventually he was holding over 1,000 patents to his name when he died."

"Yes, I guess you are right," said Karl, trying to absorb everything his father told him. He also tried to listen to the unspoken words.

"Nietzsche, on the other hand," his father continued, "allowed himself to think about the wonders of the human race and came to some astonishing conclusions. By the time he died he was known all over the world."

Karl was itching to get his five-cent comment in.

"Yeah, but Edison and Nietzsche were geniuses." There he said it.

"Right. We call people geniuses who allow themselves to use their minds. Nothing more, nothing less."

Herr Veth got up. He wanted to keep the lesson short and to the point. There was nothing gained by confusing Karl. Right now, the boy had plenty on his plate. He placed the heavy book back into the cabinet.

"To sum it up, Karl, you have to train yourself to use your mind. Look, your legs are a part of you and you use them for walking. If you train your legs for speed, you will be surprised how fast you are able to run."

"What have my legs to do with my lesson, Pappa?"

"Nothing, Karl, only that besides your legs you also have a mind. If you train it and then use is constructively you will be amazed at your own achievements."

Karl wanted dearly to comprehend what his father told him. He wanted to listen, but, like always, he had another question.

"Do all the adults train their mind and then use it correctly?"

"I don't know about other people, Karl; I can only go by what I see. It looks like that some of them are not even willing to use it to seek shelter when it rains."

FOURTEEN

Karl decided to follow the advice of his father. He went to bed and pushed the pillow into a bunch because he liked his head to be a little elevated. His father had suggested that he should gently think about his concerns and then just allow himself to drift off. He fell asleep before he even thought about the subway.

There was no answer in his head as he awoke the next morning. He took the small dynamo flashlight from his air raid suitcase and met Harold at the airshaft near the zoo station.

"You think that this one will fit?" Harold handed Karl a canister with a label of a small gasmask on the outside.

"How did you get it this fast?" Karl never ceased to be amazed at his friend's ability to produce scarce items.

"This was easy," Harold told him. "These are brand new items in my father's warehouse and for some reason he had some samples in his office. I asked him if I could exchange the masks and he told me to help myself."

"But, the mask I gave you had no storage canister," exclaimed Karl.

"This one had none either but I searched a bit because I needed a container. Look inside."

Karl opened the metal box. Right on top was an 8 oz. can of butter.

"I thought that your parents could use it in their food reserve. We have two of these cans in our emergency suitcases." Harold smiled his young innocent smile when he saw the perplexed expression on Karl's face.

"Thank you, Harold." Karl imagined what his mother might say when he handed her the canister with the butter on top of the new gasmask.

"Nothing to it," Harold assured him and produced a small

compass from his pocket. It was the regular Jungvolk-issue compass with a fold-up mirror.

"Let's see if this will do us any good," Harold pondered as the boys walked through the hallway of an apartment complex. Some of the smaller airshafts of the subway system exited in the sidewalks. Some of the larger ones were kind of concealed in the courtyards of the huge four and five-story apartment buildings. The one they wanted to use was in the very far rear court of a prestigious building on the Kurfuerstendam.

Once they were inside the tunnel they oriented themselves as to the general direction in which the trains were traveling and stepped off the distance to the mystery pathway. They took a compass bearing and stepped off the distance again. This time they directed the light to the floor. They could clearly see their own foot prints from the day before but in addition they could also see many other foot prints.

"This is unusual," ventured Karl, "most of them are going towards the end of the tunnel."

"Yes, but some of them are also walking the other way," Harold pointed out.

The boys were not experienced enough to read anything else from the tracks but Karl saw a small imprint. "This looks like a child's footprint. I wonder how old the tracks are."

"In which direction was the child going?" Harold asked.

Karl searched to find another likewise imprint, but the other overlaying shoe marks made a positive answer impossible. "Maybe this was an escape tunnel when the SS was rounding up the Jews," Karl speculated.

"Possible," allowed Harold, "but maybe the tracks are not that old and the tunnel is still active."

"Could be, but I think that the cemented metal grate speaks against it. It would, however, explain the few marks leading in the direction of the main tunnel." Karl sounded undecided. "Maybe if we could find out what is above this tunnel we would know the answer."

The boys had recorded the bearings on a piece of paper and stepped of the distance again as they went back.

On the way out Karl picked up the gasmask container he had left at the airshaft. "Let's start; about 1,900 feet along the main line and then we have to change directions." Harold agreed and the boys walked down the Kurfuerstendam and came to a stop between the famous café Kranzler and the Fernbahnhof (long distance train station) Zoologischer Garten.

"Now, let's see what lies in the direction of the compass bearing," Karl suggested. The boys could not really decide on the exact direction and Karl suggested they walk the remaining 1,200 feet and then walk in an arc. Somehow, he supposed, that they would find a building. But there was no building. Matter of fact, at the estimated distance, there were the long distance railroad tracks, city train rails and the entrance to the Zoo.

There were plenty of open spaces and small plazas in between and the large Kaiser Wilhelm Memorial Church, but nothing that would indicate an entrance or exit to an underground passage.

"Several possibilities," announced Harold after the boys gave up their search. "There could have been an exit directly before the train station. We have not gone there. Maybe the culvert was put in later on to block the tunnel and the pathway extends much further beyond." He scratched his head. "And finally, we are not experienced with a compass. Maybe we are looking in the wrong places. We should go home. It is late and I have to leave tomorrow early in the morning." Karl had to agree that a prolonged exploration above ground would not produce any different results than they had already.

"I just wondered what the purpose of the side tunnel was. Maybe when you come back to Berlin we can take it up again." He looked at Harold. "You are coming back, aren't you? I hope that you don't change your mind and stay in the Napola."

"No, I don't think that I will change my mind. They run the language courses in 6 month intervals. I expect to be back in Spring time."

Karl hated to see his friend leave but he knew that his KLV assignments would also take him away. He feared that their playtime in the U-bahn tunnels had come to an end.

"Maybe you can join me when you come back," he expressed a hopeful thought.

"Whatever comes, Karl, we will stay friends." Neither one of the boys anticipated that their friendship would last another 50 years.

Karl hurried home to show his parents what his friend had accomplished. He found his family in a somber mood. His father was laying out his black suit and his usually cheerful mother was quietly searching through the closets.

"We will have to attend a funeral service for Walter. You

remember him, he was your cousin." Karl's father announced. "His tank must have crawled over a mine. No survivors have been found."

Karl had only met his cousin a few times but he remembered him as a young daredevil. Always joyful and telling jokes Karl did not understand because they always involved girls or women. Karl remembered one or two of the jokes and he had wanted to ask his cousin to explain to him what was so funny about them. Now it was too late.

The funeral service was nothing more than a small gathering at the home of his uncle. Every one of the family members was dressed in a black suit or dress except Karl. He had no dark clothing and his mother had insisted that he wear his uniform.

When his aunt saw Karl, she was taken aback for a moment. His cousin had been only eighteen years old and his HJ uniform was folded neatly below a photograph of him. The picture showed him in the black uniform of the Panzer grenadiers.

"Let's pray that the war will be over before they draft you into service," said Karl's uncle in way of a greeting.

There was no priest or pastor present and there were no remains of Walter to be buried. It was a silent get-together of a few relatives who tried to console Karl's aunt and uncle.

Karl was astonished and at the same time disappointed as he listened to the conversation of the adults. It seemed that they were somehow relieved that there were no direct funeral costs for his aunt and uncle. The military command had sent a registered letter to the family advising them that the body of Walter had been shredded by the exploding panzer. It closed with the remark that the parents should be proud of their son who sacrificed his young life for the idea of a 1,000-year Reich. *"He gave his life for his beloved Fuehrer, Adolf Hitler."*

Below the writing was a rubber stamped signature from some military casualty registration office. Karl asked for the letter and read it twice. He realized that he could read it several more times but he would still not understand why this letter was worth dying for. There must be more to it, he reasoned with himself, because he did not want to ask the adults. They were too busy discussing the retreats of the German troops in Russia.

"I did not know that Walter had been drafted and that he was a member of the panzer forces," said Karl on the way home. He tried to remember when he last saw his cousin.

"Walter had been drafted about two months ago. But he was right away ordered to the Russian front," his father informed him.

Karl thought about Rudy and the other older HJ leaders he had met during the short time he had been in the Jungvolk. He wondered if he would see any of them again.

***

A week later he was escorting a KLV train transport of 8 and 9-year-old boys to Bavaria. His departure was on a Sunday and his parents together with his little brother and sister went with him to the railroad station to see him off. His father was in a good mood because the letter from the school administration had informed him that Karl would be back within a few weeks. He was supposed to assist the female teachers during the trip and then install some of the programs he had previously designed in his camp on the island of Usedom.

Karl had spent the evening before the trip ironing his two uniform shirts and polishing his shoes. He was proud of his handiwork. The more he ironed his own shirts the more he became proficient in it. His mother was equally proud of him. He looked sharp and snappy in his uniform and with his neat haircut.

The platform in the train station was nearly filled to capacity with parents and relatives seeing off the children. Karl was perplexed that the school officials had forgotten to name a meeting place for the teachers and the sub leaders. He had been told that there was another Jungvolk sub leader appointed to this transport.

All he could see was a large bunch of crying children and adults. The heavy locomotive was already under steam and it looked like the train was ready to be boarded. But so far nobody entered the train and no one seemed to be in charge.

"See what I mean," Karl said to his parents. "If some of the school officials would find the time to come to the departure they would see firsthand that there needs to be some planning. But, nooo, they are all senior officials, and it is Sunday, and the children are finally out of their hair. So all is good." He shook his head and looked up and down the platform to spot something like a teacher.

Herr Veth had to agree that his son had a point. He decided to write a letter to the KLV administration.

"Good bye, Schwesterchen." Karl kissed his little sister and brother and shook hands with his parents.

"I'll see you real soon," he assured his parents. "It is not as if I am drafted into the military. I'll be back before you know it."

He stepped on top of the three steps leading up to the compartments of the train and took his signal whistle out of his pocket. Three ear-piercing blows from his whistle later, another boy in uniform pressed himself forward and toward him.

"Heil Hitler, my name is Peter Zahn and I am to assist you." His salute was satisfactory and Karl liked him from the first moment he saw him. His uniform was spotless, his shoes clean and polished and his face featured a grin which seemed to reach from ear to ear. He was a good deal heavier than Karl but seemed to be of the same age.

"Heil Hitler, my name is Karl Veth. Please go to the station master of this platform and ask him if we could use his public address system."

Karl handed Peter the red and white arm sleeve of the sub leaders. He had several of them in his pocket. Compliments of Harold who somehow had connections in every direction.

While Peter fumbled to adjust his shirt sleeves an older woman in the uniform of a station master pushed herself through the crowd.

"Who blew the whistle?" she demanded to know.

"I did," answered Karl.

"Stupid kid, you almost caused the train to start moving. Let me have the whistle!"

Karl just smiled at her. "Sorry, Frau Station Master. I would really appreciate your help. I need to get the children on the train. I don't know where the teachers are. Could you please be so kind and announce to the teachers to take charge?"

The woman who was prepared for an argument was perceptibly pleased by the polite answer and request. She forgot all about the whistle and motioned to Karl to follow her.

A few minutes later the loudspeaker announced in her voice, that the teachers were to meet at the station master cubicle and that the parents should assist the children to board the train, eight children per compartment.

Shortly thereafter four women teachers, between about 30 and 40 years old, showed up at the cubicle. Karl was still a little upset that the women teachers had not acted on their own, but he figured that there was nothing to be gained by being impatient. Besides, he had no authority other than over the children and not until the train was on its way. He respectfully introduced himself to the teachers who had already heard about him and were glad to meet him. Especially the oldest one.

What had started out as a little mess gave way to a nice cooperation.

"Are your parents here at the station to see you off?" Karl inquired and looked at Peter.

"Yes, they are here. But when I heard your whistle I just left them standing and came running."

"Well, say your goodbye to them and then start in the front of the train and walk through the compartments and help the boys to get settled in. I will start in the rear and we will meet in the middle."

One of the older teachers addressed Karl. "This is our first children transport. We understand that you are experienced. Do you have any suggestions for us?"

Karl shook his head. "No, this is my first time on a train. You might find a reserved compartment. I don't know."

"Fifteen minutes to departure," came the voice over the loudspeaker.

"Where are the children to help me with my suitcases?" asked one of the younger teachers. Her high heels clicked on the stones of the platform while she walked around. She had a hard time keeping her shoulder bag from slipping down her arm while at the same time she tried to keep her hair out of her eyes.

Karl looked at her in disbelief. He thought that the teachers were supposed to help the children. Not the other way around.

"I am afraid that the children have their hands full with their own belongings. You might wish to ask the station master for help." He wanted to add that she had also the option of staying behind, but his gut told him to keep this to himself.

"This is not right," she exclaimed. "My name is Hannelore Wigand. I am a member of the NSDAP (Nazi party) and I demand help. Right Now!" she almost shouted her request for assistance. Karl was unperturbed. He decided to have a little fun with the Nazi educator.

"Right now? The train is leaving. Heil Hitler." He snapped a sharp salute in her direction and turned on his left heel. He must have done something comical because he could hear the other teachers snickering behind him.

"Ten minutes to departure. We request that the parents exit the train." The station master announced through the speaker system.

Karl could hear 'Hannelore' screaming at the other teachers for help. He wondered how this would evolve and passed close to his parents on his way to the rear of the train. He waved as he passed by and his little sister threw him a kiss. *Dang,* he thought to himself, *I have another minute* and he walked back to shake their hands once more.

"What gives with the blaring woman?" asked his father.

"Don't know, Pappa, I think she is overtaxed for her job." Karl smirked and wanted to hurry on when a remark from his mother stopped him.

"I am able to understand her rant. She is a member of the 'party' and she is entitled to be helped."

"Right," smiled Herr Veth and waved at Karl to keep on going and then turned to his wife. "Karl is right. This teacher did not pay attention or is unable to read. There were luggage carts with signs for teachers and students right at the front of the platform. You remember, we placed Karl's suitcase on one of them."

Karl's mother argued that these signs are only meant for regular 'street people' and that party members are entitled to preferred services.

"Right," repeated Herr Veth.

"Please stand back from the train. Departure is imminent."

The stationmaster repeated the same message three times and a shrill whistle signaled the locomotive crew to get going.

A second later the great hall of the railroad station reverberated from the high pitched train whistle. There was no band playing as there had been at the departure of the river boat. Children transports to the air raid safe countryside were now a regular occurrence.

FIFTEEN

Karl caught a glimpse of his family from the rear wagon. They were calmly waving in his direction but he doubted that they were actually seeing him. He walked slowly through the train towards the center. To his surprise the whole train consisted of 2nd class wagons.

The German Railroad featured, at that time, three different seating arrangements. It started with wagons which were marked 3rd class. It consisted of wooden benches without individual compartments. Then came 2nd class, which featured upholstered benches and individual compartments for six to eight people. The compartments were separated from the gangway with windows and a glass sliding door.

First class consisted of similar compartments and heavy cushioned seats with a cloth of white linen covering the headrests. Most of the regular trains in 1942 were made up of eight 3rd class wagons, two 2nd class wagons and one 1st class wagon.

To Karl's relief there were no bullies on this train who commandeered the windows as there had been on the riverboat.

"Good morning. My name is Karl. I will patrol the train throughout the entire trip. If you need any help with anything, now or later at the camp, you are more than welcome to ask me." His greeting in the individual compartments was always the same and he could see that the boys were impressed by his uniform.

When he reached the approximate center of the train he found a compartment with reserved seats for the teachers. 'Hannelore' was seated next to the gangway and still had a problem with getting her hair under control. She was sitting straight up and one of her locks covered half of her face and one of her eyes. She would wipe the hair back with her hand and a short time later her eye was covered again.

Karl was dumbfounded. He had never seen anything so bizarre. The women in his family did not have this problem and none of the other women he had met in his short lifetime suffered from a similar disorder.

He just could not help himself. "Heil Hitler," he shouted with an outstretched arm. He clicked his heels and stared directly at Hannelore's party bonbon. Bingo, her hair fell down and one of her eyes was covered again.

"I am sorry to report that we do not feature a first class compartment for party members." A blank look from Hannelore. The other female teachers could not believe their ears. They started to like the young boy.

"If you would have made your reservation early enough we might have been able to accommodate you. However, if you wish a pillow, I will endeavor to find you one." None of Karl's features gave an indication whether he was serious or if was mocking the party member.

Hannelore resolutely pushed her hair back. "I don't need a cushion, but I demand respect," she answered lamely.

Karl was on a tear and pressed on. "Frau Wigand, with all due respect, I have to warn you that you are supposed to answer my salute with a likewise 'Heil Hitler'. If you fail to do so I have orders to report you for disloyalty to the SS commander in Berlin."

The oldest teacher thought she detected some twinkle in Karl's eyes. But, if there was, it was not obvious to Hannelore. She sat stiff as a board and glared at Karl's uniform.

Karl clicked his heels, shouted once more "Heil Hitler" and left the compartment.

"I think that I will ask for a transfer," said Hannelore Wigand to the other teachers. This time she caught her hair in time.

A little bit further along the gangway, Karl bumped into Peter coming from the front of the train. "Everything alright?" he asked his new partner.

Peter grinned from ear to ear. "Everything is fine, Karl. Any specific instructions for me?"

Karl stood still for a moment and then a thought crossed his mind. He had to test his newfound friend anyhow.

"Yes there is. A few compartments back is the teacher's cubicle. I am a little intimidated by Frau Wigand. She is the teacher sitting next to the gangway. Do you remember her from the train station?"

"No," said Peter. "You sent me away before I met anyone."

"Anyhow," Karl continued, "do you know how to correctly salute a party member?

"No, but I know how to salute an officer," Peter replied.

"Good, good, it is almost the same. Except, instead of vocalizing the rank of the officer you simply say: 'Partei Genosse, (party member) and follow up with the name, if you know it. Understand?"

Peter was a bit unsure. "Please give me an example, Karl." Karl was only too glad to comply.

"Heil Hitler, Partei Genosse Wigand." He extended his arm and clicked his heels to give Peter the correct example.

"That's all?" asked Peter. "You just want me to salute her?"

"No," said Karl, "after your salute ask her if she has any special wishes. But be sure to yell real loud at her. I think she is hard of hearing. Click your heels and lock eyes with her or look straight at her party emblem."

"I don't know, Karl, this sounds a bit weird." Peter had some misgivings. He had known Karl just for a few minutes, but he could not picture him being intimidated by a female teacher or anyone else. Karl's demeanor was far too self-assured.

"Alright," Karl felt sorry for Peter who seemed to trust him. "This here is more like a private joke between us. There is no harm in it. I just don't like stupid adults."

Peter did not answer and Karl continued.

"Hmm, yes, I know there are no stupid adults, Peter. Sorry I said this. But there are adults who act stupid. You have to give me this," Karl smiled.

Peter's face brightened up again. "Don't worry Karl. If this is just a harmless joke between us, I am all for it. But why do you think that this Frau Wigand acts stupid?"

Karl shrugged his shoulders. "It is either that or she is disturbed."

"Are you saying that she is nuts?"

"No, of course not, I don't even know her. It is just ..." Karl was searching for words. "It is just that she is demanding respect and at the same time she is unable to control her hair."

"She is unable to control her hair? What's that? And this is why you want me to ask her if she has any special wishes?"

"Yes, you got it," agreed Karl. "See how harmless it is?"

Peter's eyes glazed over. "I understand nothing, Karl. But I will do it. However, you owe me one."

He walked towards the teacher's compartment. Karl followed at a safe distance. It was not in his interest to be seen by the teachers.

"Heil Hitler, Partei Genosse Wigand. Do you need anything? Or do you have any special wishes?" Karl heard Peter's voice loud and clear. Darn, Peter was alright.

There was a moment of silence and then "Heil Hitler. No, thank you." It was the voice from Frau Wigand.

Karl smiled to himself and continued his walk forward to introduce himself to the remainder of the boys and then took a seat near the front of the train. A short time later he was joined by Peter.

Before the boys could talk to each other, the seemingly oldest teacher entered their cubicle. She looked sternly at Karl. "Karl, my name is Frau Grunert. Why do you pick on Frau Wigand?"

Karl got up. "Nice to meet you, Frau Grunert. I am not picking on Frau Wigand. She wanted children to help her with her luggage and she demanded respect as a Nazi party member. I only complied with her demands. I saluted her correctly and she ignored it. I advised her according with my HJ instructions as to the consequences and sent sub leader Peter to salute her and to offer his services."

Frau Grunert was impressed by the unapologetic answer. Everything Karl had stated was true. Matter of fact, Karl had been under no obligation to warn Frau Wigand of the consequences. She had seen children ratting on their parents and she had witnessed the penalties. But still, she was supposed to be the senior teacher and leader of the camp and could not afford to lose a teacher before she even got to the camp's location.

After Peter had left the compartment, Frau Wigand had announced that she would take the next train home.

"Karl, look, you seem to be an intelligent boy. I have seen your recommendation and your report cards. Because of this I have specifically asked for you as my camp sub leader and now I need your help. Frau Wigand wants to get back to Berlin and we need her as a teacher."

"How many children do we have in this camp?" asked Karl.

"Close to three hundred," answered Frau Grunert.

"Alright, if you are down to three teachers you will have a class size of about one hundred students. From what I have seen this is doable."

He took his seat again because Frau Grunert was sitting down by the window.

"What do you wish me to do, or how would like me to help you?"

"I want you to talk to Frau Wigand. Tell her that you will not report her. She might change her mind and stay with us."

Karl smiled. "I'd be happy to talk to her and convince her to stay. I will also assure her that she is safe from me. Besides, I would never report anyone." It was easy for him to give this assurance because it was true.

"But, tell me Frau Grunert. Are we really this short of educators that we need someone like Frau Wigand as a teacher?"

"What do you mean, Karl?"

"Frau Wigand is enthralled with herself. She stumbles around on high heels, she is fighting with her shoulder bag and can't keep her hair out of her eyes. In spite of this she is demanding respect. For what? Nine-year-old boys are not that stupid. They will see right through her and know that they cannot learn anything worthwhile from a teacher like that."

Frau Grunert was forced to defend her teacher. "What possessed you to come from her behavior to this startling conclusion?"

"I am training myself to connect the dots. I agree in Frau Wigand's case I have only very few dots to connect. But still, they are enough to support my assumption."

Karl took a piece of paper and a pencil from his pocket. He straightened out the folds and marked four dots on the paper. Two of them above the other two, they were of about equal distance to each other.

"Please look at this, Frau Grunert." He connected the dots and showed her a square. "This is not a circle, this is not a triangle, this is a square. Not much doubt about it. Maybe not a perfect square, but it is pretty close to one." Karl put his pencil away.

"Karl, your drawing looks convincing but you cannot compare a person's ability with the outline of a few dots." Frau Grunert asserted. She had to admit to herself that the square did not resemble a triangle and kept looking at the paper.

"You are right, Frau Grunert. I am new and inexperienced at this concept of connecting the dots. Please show me where I am wrong."

While Karl politely agreed with Frau Grunert, Peter was captivated by the dialog. He had thought that Frau Grunert would put Karl on the defensive; instead it seemed that his new friend was constantly scoring points.

"I cannot show you that your drawing is a circle, but at the same time your square is no indication of Frau's Wigand's ability or inability as a teacher." Frau Grunert was adamant. "A human being is a complex entity and cannot be defined by a few dots and pencil strokes."

"You are right again, Frau Grunert. We need a few more dots."

There was a knock on the door and a boy stuck his head into the cubicle. "My name is Dieter. We were promised some sandwiches or something to eat. Where do we get it?"

Frau Grunert got up. "Thanks for reminding us. Please go back to your place. We will come with some trays in a minute. I think we even have some cookies for you." She motioned at Peter and Karl. "Come with me and we will serve the children together."

Karl also got up and put the paper back in his pocket. He opened the sliding door for the senior teacher. "Please don't worry about Frau Wigand. I will talk to her," he promised her again.

The boys followed her to the teacher's cubicle. Hannelore frowned at the boys who stood in the doorframe when Frau Grunert entered.

"We should tend to the food service. Where are the boxes with the sandwiches?" she asked and looked from one teacher to the other.

Everybody shrugged their shoulders and looked at each other. Frau Grunert's face changed to a slight shade of red. "Everybody had specific orders. Who was responsible for getting the food on the train?" she demanded. She reached into her handbag and took out a typed manual. It listed the names of the teachers and their individual duties. Before she could ascertain who was in charge of the food detail Frau Wigand spoke up.

"There was just too much of a hurry and confusion at the station. I remember now that it was my job. But there was not enough time. I had to look out for my belongings."

Before Frau Grunert could think of an answer, Peter piped up. "I saw some brown cardboard boxes at the front of the platform. They were marked KLV rations. I thought that they belonged on the train, so I placed them in an empty compartment on the first wagon."

All of the faces showed immediate relief except Frau Wigand's.

"See, this is what I mean. Everybody was busy doing something. No wonder that I could not keep track of everything." Her hair covered again half of her face.

Karl said nothing. He reached into his pocket and while he

looked keenly at Frau Grunert, he added another dot to his drawing. He was just about to put it back in his pocket when it seemed that he remembered something. He turned the paper around and wrote something on the backside.

"What are you doing, Karl," asked Frau Grunert, who had watched him while the other teachers followed Peter to the front of the train.

"I am starting another diagram," said Karl.

"Why?" demanded Frau Grunert. "Isn't adding a dot enough for your conclusions?"

"It is," agreed Karl. "The one on the backside is for Peter."

"Karl," said the senior teacher. "The very moment we are settled in our camp I want to see you in my office. You and I need to talk." She smiled at him as she said it and the tone of her voice was warm and friendly. Karl could sense that it would be a pleasant meeting.

***

The camp was near Stallwang in the BavAryan forest and the sleeping quarters of the boys were divided between several farms. Frau Grunert turned out to be a very competent camp leader and Karl enjoyed his frequent conversations with her.

He had also talked with Frau Wigand with the result that she reconsidered and stayed on as a teacher for the six-month term of the camp. Karl, on the other hand had not revised his initial impression of her. He had no reason to do so. She shirked any kind of work not directly related to teaching. Peeling potatoes or even the cleaning of her own room was strictly beneath her.

"How do you obtain a teaching degree?" he had asked Frau Grunert in the second month of their stay. "You cannot receive it by setting an example, because Frau Wigand would have flunked it."

"Listen, Karl, you are much too harsh in your expectations. We are in extremely serious times and facing serious conditions. You should give Frau Wigand and also yourself a lot more leeway."

Karl considered the answer because he wanted to learn from this knowledgeable camp leader. She might be right, he thought. I should be more flexible.

"You are right, as always, Frau Grunert. I think that giving others and myself more latitude makes for a much easier and also pleasant living." He tried to picture himself lying lazily in the sun and not caring what was going on around him or what was coming down the pike. However, that was not him and he could not really imagine himself doing that.

"Tell me, Frau Grunert. These marginally competent teachers, I mean the ones who are only concerned about themselves and don't care about being a good role model for the children, can't they just be dismissed by the school administrators and forced to leave the school system? And if not, are they receiving the same pay as the really proficient teachers, like you?"

Frau Grunert was surprised by the blunt question.

"No Karl, we cannot throw teachers on the street and yes, we all receive the same pay, subject to the length of our teaching career."

Karl nodded his head. "If this is the case, then you are right. We are not only facing serious conditions, we are experiencing them right now."

He went to see Peter who was in the middle of organizing something like a soccer match between two teams. Karl admired Peter's dedication to team sports. This was something he could not get excited about. That he should cheer for one team or the other did not make any sense to him. One team had to win, no way around it, but the next time the other team would win. So what was the big deal?

"Karl, I think I know the reason why you don't like team sports," Peter ventured when he saw Karl on the side lines.

"Alright, Doctor Peter, please tell me." Karl mirrored Peters grin.

"I think that you are not competitive," Peter decided.

"You know what, Peter? I think that you are right. I mean, I like to succeed, but not at the expense of someone else."

"Come on, Karl, you are not a saint," Peter teased him.

"No, I am definitely not. And I like to learn. One of these days you have to teach me how to chase after a ball without falling flat on my face."

"I will," promised Peter. "In the meantime what are you up to right now? Frau Grunert told me that you had some thoughtful phone calls with Berlin. Does this have something to do with the reports you are writing for the HJ monthlies?"

"No, Peter, I am trying to get some replacements for us. I would like you to return with me to Berlin. We have the camp here in a very good shape. I hear from the school administration that they have some issues in other camps. Maybe we can stay together and solve some of their challenges."

"I would like that very much," replied Peter.

SIXTEEN

A few weeks later, Karl was summoned to Berlin. When he returned he had two other boys with him. Both of them were 14 years old and members of the HJ. One was a rather likeable fellow named Franz. The other's name was Albert and he had a round face like a full moon. He was full of himself and exhibited a rash superior attitude towards Karl, who could not care less.

Karl knew that he had initiated all the main activities in the Stallwang camp while Albert was merely stepping into an orderly structure.

Peter was pleasantly surprised when Karl announced on his return that they only had three days to instruct Albert and Franz into the intricacies of running an orderly camp. After that, Peter would enjoy a few days with his parents and then join Karl on his next assignment.

"Please do me a favor, Karl. Why don't you take fat head Albert under your wing while I work with Franz. You have much more patience than I have. I can't stand the smug expression on Albert's face. I don't know why, but every time I see him I feel like punching him in the nose."

Karl laughed. "No problem, Peter. I owe you one anyhow, remember?"

Peter shook his head. "You do?"

"Yes," Karl assured him, "think back to the train ride."

Karl made his way to Frau Grunert who did not at all like the idea that Karl was leaving the camp. She had called the school administrator several times and even went so far as calling the KLV officials who had redirected her call to the school superintendent.

"Well, Frau Grunert" he had replied. "If you are so convinced of Karl Veth's abilities, then this is just one more reason for us to send him on to the camps which need him more than you do. Be happy that we did not recall him earlier. Heil Hitler." End of conversation and of her appeal.

Karl knew none of this when he went to ask Frau Grunert if she had any final requests.

"No, Karl, other than I wish you would stay with us. Your connections to Berlin must be pretty potent, because I wanted to keep you here. I wish you luck in all of your endeavors."

"Thank you, Frau Grunert. I don't know anything about my connections. I just write reports and offer suggestions. But I really appreciate your kind wishes for my future. Maybe we will see each other again. Right now I am staying for another three days to assist Albert and Franz."

He had taken one look at Albert and had speculated that this guy must be constantly hungry to support his outsized face. He was right. Albert displayed an enormous appetite. But food was becoming more and more a rare commodity and it was very seldom that the children had a chance for a second helping.

"Albert, if you feel like having an extra sandwich, why don't you see me after you unpack," he told the bigger boy and went back to observe Peter and Franz with their soccer practice.

In spite of Frau Wigand's blunder on the first day on the train, she was in charge of the camp's food provisions and Karl planned to use this point to obtain some cooperation from Albert.

"You said something about a sandwich." Albert showed up within a few minutes after Karl had teased him.

"Yes, Albert. I noticed that the rations are a little too meager for your size. Of course if you know your way around, then this will not be a problem for you." He handed him a sandwich which he had saved for this purpose.

"What do you mean 'if I know my way around'?" Albert asked as he took a hearty bite.

'Well," said Karl, "if you work with me closely during the few days we have together you will see for yourself what I mean."

Albert promised to pay attention and he cooperated as well as he could during the next days. But as much as he tried, he was unable to detect how Karl was able to get his hands on the extra food.

Karl's solution was not that complicated and dated a few weeks back when he had initiated the kitchen duty details. Every evening a different group of boys cleaned up the food preparation area. Actually, it was in teacher Wigand's job description to clean the food storage and the kitchen facility. Karl had right away seen that this was another chore below the dignity of the hair-impaired Hannelore.

He had smilingly offered a deal she could not refuse. He promised her that his boys would do a super cleanup job if she would look the other way if there was ever a loaf of bread missing or some other minor edibles. He explained to her that this was necessary to assure that the boys would do an impeccable job.

Teacher Wigand agreed but added one condition, the boys were also to clean her personal room. She asked Karl to keep this arrangement quiet. It suited him fine. As long as his kitchen detail was compensated with food, he had no problem using teacher Wigand's laziness to the boys' advantage.

On the last evening before his departure he let Albert in on the arrangement.

"Teacher Wigand wants our boys to clean her room?" exclaimed Albert.

"Psss," answered Karl, "what do you care as long as you are getting an extra sandwich in the evening?"

"As long as I don't have to do the actual cleaning." Albert wanted to be sure.

"No, you don't have to do the cleaning, but you have to be very deferential to Frau Wigand. She is a Nazi member and expects to be respected."

"What do you mean by that? You are not suggesting that I should serve her every whim?"

"No, no," Karl assured him, "she just likes to be saluted. Keep it real snappy and loud." Karl lowered his voice as if to let Albert in on a secret. "I think she is a bit deaf. Better you know it now than later."

"Oh, if this is all that is required, she will be pleased how loud I am able to shout 'Heil Hitler'. Tell me if this is satisfactory." Before Karl had a chance to stop the moon face, Albert threw his arm in the air and shouted his salute loud enough to make it sound like a scream.

"Perfect, Albert. But don't forget to add her name. She really dwells on it."

"Thank you, Karl. I will salute her every time I pass her. Funny how some of the party people get off on it."

Karl agreed and handed him next week's schedule of the work details. "Hmm, there is another thing you should know. Frau Grunert, the camp leader, is just the opposite. She might not even like it when you greet Frau Wigand loud and often. Don't be deterred by it. I mean, if you like the sandwiches coming your way." He winked one eye at the moon face who understood. He winked back.

***

Karl and Peter left early the next morning and Karl did not have a chance to observe Albert's actions. He did, however, hear from the KLV headquarters that Frau Grunert demanded that Albert be replaced.

Once back in Berlin, Karl reported immediately to his school superintendent and the Jungvolk Dienststelle, or office.

It was shortly before Christmas and the boys hoped that they could spend it at home. The KLV officials, however, had different plans. For several reasons they needed the boys badly. The school evacuation was now mandatory. But in spite of the German discipline, it took more than 18 months to get it fully organized.

First of all there was an extreme shortage of teachers. All of the able male teachers had been drafted and the older ones served in management positions in the ammunition and armament factories. Most of the female teachers were not inclined to take on class sizes in excess of 100 students. They simply joined the Nazi party to receive preferential treatment.

Second, this preferential treatment for members of the Nazi party applied not only to the teachers, but also for the children of Nazi officials.

Third, the camps themselves had to get organized. Farms were the first choice and then came the so-called resorts. Local school buildings and police stations in the country were used as dormitories and filled beyond their capacity. However, as the air attacks and casualties of the children in the targeted cities increased, severe and drastic measures were needed and instigated. It was during this time of transition that Karl and Peter were shuffled back and forth between the new camps and the KLV administration in Berlin.

They were not the only ones. There were several other sub leader teams just as active. The major difference in the other teams was the age of Karl and Peter. Both had finished the elementary school requirements two years ahead of their classmates. The other teams were not only older (14 and 15 years old) they were also expected to stay with the camp once it was established. It was Karl's ability to write accurate reports and to relate to the children as well as to the parents and school officials that he was tasked as being more or less a trouble shooter.

In a way he was glad to have the sports-oriented Peter as his teammate. He knew Harold better and longer, but Harold was at the Napola and Peter was perfect for installing physical fitness programs for the 8 to 10-year-old kids. Harold on the other hand was like Karl. He would have been unwilling to exercise or play with a stupid ball.

"Karl, I want you to talk to a group of parents tonight. You should know that these are all high ranking Nazi members. Keep your comments strictly to the essentials."

Karl was in the KLV headquarters building. It was the first week of December and it was bitter cold. The building was not heated and he shivered as he listened to the new administrator. It was a former artillery officer with no experience in school administration matters, but Karl did not know that.

"Any particular aspect you want me to address?" He did not need any time to prepare for the meeting but maybe the Nazi group had specific interests.

"No, but I need you to assure the parents that their children will be well cared for. None of them want their children to leave before Christmas, but due to logistics we have to move them out next week."

"How old are the students and from what school district?"

"They are between 8 and 9 years old and not from a specific school. You need to be here at exactly 6:00 PM."

"Not an issue, Herr Hartung." Karl looked at the name plate on the desk. The administrator extended his hand to say goodbye. His suit showed no party emblem and Karl wondered how this able-looking man was exempt from the service.

"I don't know if anyone told you, but you and Peter are assigned to the transport."

"No, Herr Hartung, we just returned from the BavAryan Forest and hoped to spend Christmas with our parents." Karl was disappointed.

"Maybe I can bring you home for a few days, but don't count on it." The administrator pushed himself away from the desk and Karl saw that he was sitting in a wheelchair. Another war casualty being recycled.

Karl felt an impulse to salute but Herr Hartung waved him off.

"Thanks for the gesture, Karl. These times are behind me. Just be on time."

Karl could see in the posture of Herr Hartung that he must have been an officer. At first he wondered about the un-patriotic answer but then he figured that a person without legs might not be scared of a political repercussion.

When he arrived in the evening he was seated in a meeting hall close to the podium. The first teacher to address the audience of over 200 parents was a nicely dressed elderly woman. She assured the parents that the children would be very well taken care of. She mentioned the current meager food rationing in Berlin and promised that the children would receive three meals a day. It seemed to Karl that the parents were glad to hear that.

The next teacher spoke about the overall educational aspect by having the young children exposed to a different lifestyle in the country. She also said that the children would be happy to be away from the bombings and the destruction. Most of all they would love their new surroundings and never even miss their parents or the family. Karl wondered where she got this idea from.

Another teacher spoke about the daily hygiene in the camp and the need for adequate clothing.

Karl was the last one to address the parents. It was not in his interest to discredit the teachers but it bothered him that they had not addressed a very basic need of the students.

"My name is Karl. I have been a sub leader since the very first KLV camp was initiated. I live with them and I understand their needs."

He paused for a moment to step away from the podium. "Please ask me questions about the actual camp life."

For about 15 minutes he fielded various questions from the food quality to the leisure time activities. His answers made it very clear to the audience that he spoke from actual experience.

"Now, do you wish to know what the KLV camp is unable to provide but what we, as the children, need the most?" All of the parents seem to agree that this might be important and encouraged him to continue.

"This is not a long lecture. I can sum it up in five words." All looked up to him. Even the teachers wanted to hear the magic words.

"We need letters from home."

All the parents and relatives in the audience seemed to think that this was a given and replied that off course they would write to their children. But, Karl was not done. Not by a long shot.

"Yes, you write, but not nearly enough. Please imagine yourself being 8 years old, unable to sleep at night because you don't know what you did wrong. Your classmates received a letter and you did not." There was a loud murmur from the crowd but stopped again as Karl continued.

"Picture yourself in the shoes of your child being worried that something might have happened to you." A teacher spoke up to defend the parents, saying that it is impossible to write every day, besides the postal service is interrupted from time to time and mail gets lost because of damage to the postal facilities.

Karl was undeterred. "I am not done." He informed the teacher.

"I sleep with the children and therefore know what I am talking about. The issues you raised are no longer valid because I addressed them in the last camp and I hope that they will get initiated in all the camps."

It seemed that the teacher took Karl's answer personal.

"So you eliminated the damage to the postal service!" She nearly shouted.

Before Karl could answer, Herr Hartung intervened. "Let Karl finish, if he says that he has addressed the problem we should at least listen to him." He waved at Karl to continue.

"Thank you," said Karl, "I realized that the mail service was erratic and I placed all incoming mail on hold until Wednesday mornings. This way there is only one mail call per week and delayed letters have a chance to catch up. It also resulted in a much better mail call. Nearly all the children received a letter. It is the parents or relatives who don't find the time to write once a week that I wish to remind how it feels when you realize that no one cares for you."

"Why Wednesdays?" Herr Hartung asked who started to feel uncomfortable.

"We initiated enough leisure activities to make the weekend interesting and something to look forward too. By deciding on Wednesday I broke up the week."

The administrator nodded his approval.

"One more thing, please." Karl was indeed not finished.

"Go ahead, Karl." The teacher who had so rudely interrupted Karl before was all of the sudden interested in what else he might have to say.

Karl looked over the listeners. "I wish that I could force you to do this, but because I can't, I need your voluntary help. Please give your children stamps and pre-addressed envelopes to take along with them. I initiated a 'write to home' evening on Wednesday night and on Sunday night. Some of the children don't have stamps or the money to buy any. It would also be nice if the parents would give a small amount, like maybe five Marks (German currency unit) to the children. This would allow me to take a group of students on an outing to the local stationary store and they would be able to purchase a picture postcard to send home."

When Karl sat down he received a nice applause. Several of the parents came up to his chair to talk to him. Again he fielded all the questions to the best of his knowledge and by the time he was leaving he had a whole breast pocket full of addresses from individual parents who wanted him to pay special attention to their son.

This was kind of new to Karl and he decided to never attend another parent meeting without having Peter or some other sub leader on his side. There was no way that he could possibly fulfill the expectations by himself.

He wished that the parents and relatives would approach the teachers with their requests. However, the teachers conducting the meetings were seldom the ones who went along to the relevant camp.

Many of the camp teachers were the local teachers of the towns where the camp was located.

SEVENTEEN

When Karl was leaving he was stopped by the KLV administrator. "Karl, I think that you woke up some parents. I will add a comment in your file. Goodnight."

Karl was happy. It was the first time that he had spoken to a group of nearly 200 people. He had simply followed his father's advice from a few months ago. He had allowed himself to think that it was possible for him to speak to a large audience. And it was.

"How did it go?" his parents asked when he sat down at the supper table. Karl was excited and told them all about the evening.

"I enjoyed it. I did not know that I could do that. Thank you, Pappa."

"Congratulations, son. Don't forget to build on what you learned tonight. Think about how many children will be affected. They will never know that it was you and your words they have to be thankful for when they receive an extra letter from home, but they will surely enjoy it."

It was past 10:00 PM when Karl went to sleep. He was happy that Herr Hartung had indicated that he might be home for Christmas. Nobody had told him anything about the new camp's location and he hoped that it was in a different part of the country he had been before. He was starting to love traveling.

This was a good thing too because during the next 12 months he and his teammate Peter were ordered to visit camps throughout Germany and also through a part of Poland. Their instructions were mostly the same: look for deficiencies and install order in camps where the smaller children were ruled by bullies. While Karl was concerned with the daily hygiene, Peter was charged with instilling order when some unruly boys tried to rule the camp.

In the beginning it was a somewhat difficult assignment. Many of the intimidators were not only physically stronger than their classmates but they had also caught on that they could get away with almost anything by threatening the teachers.

Karl could see that there seemed to be a common denominator. Either the tormentors were children of highly placed Nazi members or they had an older brother or other relative who had told the kid that he could get what he wanted by threatening the teachers with reporting them as dissidents to the SS.

The threat alone was sufficient.

Karl shared his observations with Peter and the boys came to a simple conclusion. Well, it was not exactly simple because it took some groundwork but after a trip to the HJ headquarters in Berlin and explaining his difficulties to the Jungvolk leaders who were in charge of the sport programs, he had the green light to proceed.

"Let's go and talk to the local HJ office," Karl announced upon his return from Berlin. It turned out that the local units were only too happy to assist. They arranged with the local children many minor sport competition games with the camp. This was a big deal for the bullies of the camp who wanted to assert themselves right from the start. However, now they were not only up against their own age group but also against older kids. The local boys were in the minority compared to the camps but the older ones prevailed in scoring points, badges and trophies. Since age did not matter in the competition and the games were designed to further the natural abilities of the boys, it turned out to be a valid struggle to maintain any possible lead. Pretty soon the whole camp was a united force. Almost overnight, the formerly unruly boys became the able leaders of the camp children.

Peter was a master in devising competition games which ranged from soccer to long-distance team running with several balls, sometimes up to two or three miles without stopping or rotating the balls.

"I like our arrangement," Peter told Karl. "You are most welcome to teach the children to clean up the bathrooms while I am enjoying with them the fresh air." He threw a handball in Karl's direction. It bounced off his friends head as he was trying to catch it.

"Leave me alone," pleaded Karl. "I have my hands full to get them to brush their teeth, never mind cleaning the toilets."

"Yeah, I agree, but this is no excuse for not being able to catch a ball." He bounced another ball off Karl's head.

"Ouch," complained Karl, "you hit me right on my forehead."

Peter shrugged his shoulders. "Of course I hit you on the forehead; you are standing right in front of me."

As Karl went for cover he mumbled something about brawny bodies with underdeveloped brains, but he did not mean it. He liked Peter.

***

Because of the constant challenges and varying locations, the next 12 months passed quickly. By the time Christmas 1943 approached they had enough support from the KLV administration to spend a week home with their parents.

Peter's family lived in Stralau, a suburb from Berlin. Karl hoped to introduce him to Harold, who had completed his second language course. However, Harold's grandparents had invited their grandson to spend the Christmas week at their small house by Hamburg and Karl was unable to see him before the holidays.

He spent the last day before Christmas Eve trying to memorize a festive poem to surprise his grandparents. It was a tradition in the Veth's family that they spend Christmas Eve by themselves at home. However on Christmas Day, they would visit grandfather Veth and on the second Christmas Day (Christmas consisted of two days in Germany) they would be home again. They never visited Karl's mother's parents. That's the way it was for as long as Karl could remember.

Another tradition was that the children received their presents on Christmas Eve. Karl wanted to surprise his parents with a present of his own and had been able to secure a small glass salad bowl with two serving spoons as a present for his mother. He had no wrapping paper and used a white towel to make it somewhat presentable. Then he took a plain sheet of writing paper and printed in big letters: '*For our beloved mother*' he signed it '*Karl*' and then gave it to his 6-year-old brother, who had just learned to write his name. However, little 3-year-old Monika just doodled something below her brothers' signatures.

When they were done Karl scrutinized the paper and decided that something was missing. He asked his brother for a green crayon and drew something resembling a pine tree branch on top of the letter. His drawing was awful. It did not look like a pine tree at all, so he asked his brother for more crayons to draw some colored Christmas balls on the branch. When he went into the bedroom to find another towel to wrap up the present for his father, his brother used the opportunity to draw some Christmas balls of his own and then handed it to Monika to finish the Christmas letter.

By the time Karl was back and able to pin the paper to the present it was a jumble of colors and even the original writing was hard to decipher. There was not enough time to do it over again so Karl reached for a pencil and wrote on the side: 'Christmas branch' and drew an arrow pointing to the green lines resembling nothing.

The wrapping for his father's present, which was a wastepaper basket, was more difficult. Karl had seen wastepaper baskets at the various offices of the KLV administration and he thought that his dad might like to have one. The money for the presents came from the gratuities he sometimes received from various parents.

After Karl finished wrapping the basket he wrote again *'For our beloved Pappa"* on a sheet of paper. This time he just signed his name and wrote underneath *'for the other signatures please turn over'*.

He gave the paper with the blank side up to his brother.

"Here, Willy, express yourself."

When he got it back, Willy and Monika had 'expressed themselves' on both sides of the letter. Karl looked at it with some dismay but then decided that it was 'original' and left it the way it was.

"Don't open the presents," Karl told his mother as he gave them to her in the bedroom. The Christmas tree was set up by his mother in the living room and none of the children were allowed to see it. Like every year, the Christkindchen (Christmas child) arrived exactly at 7 PM.

Neither Karl, Willy nor Monika had ever seen him arrive, but nevertheless the door to the living room opened on time and the children were allowed to enter. In the corner of the room stood a nice Christmas tree around 4-feet tall on a table. It was decorated with Lametta (tin foil) and colored Christmas balls. Karl was deeply surprised and astonished. His father was very modern and surprised his family with the first electric Christmas light set Karl had ever seen. It consisted of 16 white light bulbs in the shape of regular candles.

It was a beautiful moment when the children cast their eyes on the tree. Each of them received two shiny green apples and some cookies and a tiny bar of chocolate. Monika received a Kate Kruse

Puppe (doll) with imitation hair. Willy received a wooden train set and Karl was happy when he saw several books.

Karl wondered where his parents had obtained the chocolate. It must have been magic because there was none available in the stores. After the family sang 'Silent Night' the children were allowed to sit down. Karl wanted to bury his head in a book written by Gunther Prien, a famous German submarine commander, when his father announced that he had another surprise for them. It was 8:00 PM and he turned on the radio.

After the usual OKW report, the reporter announced a special transmission from the city of Cologne. For 15 minutes the family listened to the wonderful deep sound of the church bells from the famous Cologne Dom (Cathedral). While the ringing of the bells was transmitted over the radio waves, the local church bells in Berlin chimed in. In spite of the cold winter night, Karl's mother opened the window for a minute so that they could also hear the sound of the Ludwig church bells.

After the last sound of the gigantic church bell diminished everyone was quiet to savor the festive moment. In the spirit of Christmas, Herr Veth announced to the family that they were allowed to listen to another hour of a music program.

"Do you remember your Christmas poem?" Karl questioned Willy on the next day. He was itching to see his grandfather again and he was wondering if his little brother was ready to visit the grandparents.

"No," said Willy. "Mutti said that if I make an honest Christmas promise, I don't have to recite a poem."

This was news for Karl. A long as he could remember back, he had always been asked by his parents to please the grandparents on Christmas day with a selected verse.

"What kind of a promise will you make?" he wondered.

"No, I will not tell you. It will be a surprise," declared Willy. He was like Karl, ready for the short walk to the grandparent's apartment. The Christmas day visit was nothing short of an annual ceremony and Karl was prepared and eager to get started.

"Merry Christmas," announced his father after the grandma had opened the door to their small hallway.

Karl and Willy had to wait in the hallway, which was only lit by a small light bulb, while his parents and Monika were allowed to enter the living room. After several minutes the grandfather walked through the foyer and like every year, he was carrying two pails of water. One in each hand.

"Get ready to shout 'Merry Christmas', after we are done singing," Karl reminded his brother just before a small bell sounded from the living room giving the boys the signal to enter.

Slowly the door opened and Karl reached for his brother's hand as they walked in. The grandparents, attired in their best garments, sat in two chairs on one side of a 6-foot pine tree, which was decorated with a few shiny silver balls. On the other side stood Karl's parents with little Monika between them.

It was cozy and warm in the living room. In the corner stood a huge tiled Kamin (oven to heat a room). Grandpa had stoked it with coals since the morning and the tiles radiated the heat throughout the apartment.

As the boys walked closer to the tree their grandparents started to sing O Tannenbaum (Oh Christmas tree) and Karl, Willy and their parents chimed in. Karl scanned the small bench on the far side of the room. It was covered with Christmas-colored dishes. By tradition each of the children would receive a dish of their own, which featured some apples and nuts and cookies.

Besides the dishes Karl could discern some presents for his brother and sister and to his joy he also spotted two books which were surely meant for him. His eyes wandered back and forth between the presents and the candles on the tree.

He always feared that the tree might burst into flames because of the real wax candles burning between the dried out branches but it never happened. In reality, his grandparents were not taking any chances with the burning candles. Depending upon the size of the tree, they never numbered more than nine and the two buckets of water his grandfather had provided were standing close by.

After singing the first verse, Karl let go of his brother's hand, took a step forward and recited his poem. As he delivered the second verse his grandmother did not seemed to be very pleased. It was a modern poem and had been approved by the HJ leadership. The text had something to do with stars forming a bridge in the sky to allow the souls of the fallen soldiers to communicate with their loved ones at home.

Karl liked it because it was up to date with the war going on but he had the feeling that his grandma thought it was not religious enough. However, his grandfather and his parents smiled and encouraged him to keep going. After he was done he bowed his head towards his grandparents and then stepped back to take his place next to his brother.

The grandparents started to sing the second verse of the Christmas tree song but nobody except the old cavalry officer knew all the words. Before the song ended everyone was singing the first verse again.

Karl's favorite Christmas carol was actually 'Silent Night' and he would have loved to sing it. But, of course, there was only one holy night, December 24th, and that was last evening. To sing this song on Christmas day or on any other day was unthinkable.

It was now Willy's turn to please the grandparents. Karl silently wished his brother good luck and was startled when he heard what Willy had to say.

"I will be nice," he promised and looked longingly at the cookie dish under the tree.

"And what else?" prompted his mother. Willy tried hard to think of another thing to promise. "I will share my toys with Monika."

He shifted his weight from one leg to the other. It was obvious that he wanted the cookies and that he was also at the end of his list for promises. His sister must have understood what he was saying because she started to look around for toys but was unable to see them.

The grandfather knew that it was time to let the children sit down. He got up from his chair to extinguish the candles, which were now almost halfway burned down. He fetched a strange-looking contraption to stub out the candles. It was a long stick with hooded piece of metal on the end to snuff the flame. The device also featured a wick below the hood to light any candles that were out of reach.

The living room was also the dining room and Grandma had decked the table with porcelain dishes that were only used on Sundays and only by the adults. The children had to use the regular every day earthenware dishes. Karl looked forward to the day that he would be allowed to drink out of one of the precious cups because his mother had told him once how much better the liquid tasted when it was served in the correct dishes. However, today was not the day. Grandmother served him the coffee ersatz (imitation coffee) in the regular everyday cup.

Sunday dishes and Sunday flatware for the adults, and the smell from the pine tree and the candles; it was Christmas alright. Despite the meager portions it was a festive afternoon.

"Are you thinking about buying a radio?" Herr Veth asked his father.

"I don't think that we will ever buy one," answered grandpa. "There is no reason why we should. We get all the news by reading the morning paper." He reached for yesterday's issue because there was no newspaper edition on Christmas Day. There would be also no edition on the following day. Christmas in Germany was a true two-day holiday. Everybody stayed home and all the stores were closed. Not even a pub was allowed to be open.

The street cars and buses ran during the daytime on a very limited schedule and in the evenings everything came to a total stand still.

The grandfather seemed to be looking for a particular news story but could not find it. He put the paper next to the oven where it would serve as kindling when needed.

"Do you think that you get your money's worth out of the radio you bought?" he asked his son.

"I think that would depend on how much value you place on receiving timely news about the war." Herr Veth was a little defensive because he knew that his father would never listen to anything else on the radio. Not that there was much else being transmitted. There were only two stations to choose from. One of the stations occasionally had some music programs and the other station transmitted war-related reports. Sponsors or advertisers were against the law and if they would have been permitted, nobody would have bought the advertised items in the first place.

If anything smacked of promotion it had to be an inferior product to begin with.

"Then I am right that I don't need one of these expensive toys. The war is lost anyway and if I hear about it today or read about it tomorrow in the paper, it will not matter one way or another."

The grandfather did not mention anything about the newest radios which featured a short wave receiver. They were extremely expensive and almost impossible to obtain. But they would enable a listener to obtain broadcasts from other countries in Europe and even from oversea stations. However, listening to these stations was strongly forbidden and if a citizen was caught he would face draconic penalties.

EIGHTEEN

Karl was supposed to leave with a new transport of children within the first week of January 1944. He used the free time to visit with Harold at the Jungvolk head office. It was a new office located in an office/apartment building.

"How are you coming with your English lessons?" he inquired.

"Fairly well but I am not going back for a third term."

"You mean to tell me that you are already proficient in your language skills?"

"No, not by a long shot. My schooling got suspended for the time being."

"Who suspended you? Are you out of the Napola?" Karl wondered.

"Well, my father used his influence to get me a temporary assignment as a supply clerk in the local HJ office."

"Where will this be?"

"Right here," Harold was proud to announce. "My father told me that any requisition from the local KLV and HJ district will get processed through this office."

"Interesting, but I still don't understand." Karl wanted to hear more details.

"I am not too sure myself. But, if I understand correctly, there are separate supply and food warehouses in and around the city and there are daily demands from various organizations."

The clueless expression on Karl's face did not change.

"Our office will be coordinating the requests with the available supplies," Harold tried to explain.

"So, if I get this right, you will be one of the decision makers of who gets what?"

"No, you dummy, I am only supposed to help with the paper work." Harold did not add that his father was one of the decision makers.

"When did this happen?" Karl pondered what he had just heard.

"Well, my birthday is in a few days and I will have to join the HJ. My father doesn't want me to be trained as a soldier. I think that he wants me to be a paper pusher, just like him."

"Your father must have a lot of authority to pull this off." Karl knew that the latest HJ requirements were nothing short of infantry exercises, including specific air raid emergency duties and first aid training. He would also be turning fourteen in July and hoped that his current assignment to the KLV camps would continue when he had to join the HJ.

"No, I don't think that my father has this much pull," Harold chuckled. "I think that my father is bribing the right people."

Karl was eager to hear more about the bribing technique and was ready to ask questions when the office door opened and Peter walked in. He had an appointment with Karl at the KLV office in the school building next door.

"Let's go. We are late," he urged, after Karl had introduced him to Harold.

"Will you still be here when we come back from the meeting?" Karl wanted to visit some more with his friend, who he had not seen for nearly a year.

"Don't worry, I am here to stay. I will be waiting for you." He waved at the boys as they scampered out of the door.

The meeting with the KLV officials was brief. They were informed that their destination was a newly established camp by Goslar in the Harz Mountains. A little more than three hours by train, they were told. The date of their departure was still the same, only their assembly point had been changed to a different railroad station.

Each of the boys received a packet of instructions and, to their surprise, they also received an envelope with extra rationing coupons and entitlement certificates. They were allowed to use the rationing coupons any way they wished but the entitlement certificates were for the specific items the boys had requested upon their return from the last camp.

Karl had two coupons for two pairs of long warm uniform pants and one coupon for a pair of leather winter shoes. He looked at Peter, who had a similar certificate for shoes, and both of them wondered where they could possibly buy their footwear. All the regular clothing stores and shoe stores were nearly empty of merchandise.

"Where do we go shopping with these papers?" Peter asked the KLV clerk who shook his head.

"I don't know, besides these certificates you also need certain Beziehungen (connections) but don't look at me. I don't have any."

"What now?" Peter looked at Karl. "Do you have any connections?"

"Not really and not to any stores," Karl twirled the certificates in his hand. "But we might know someone who does."

They walked back to the Jungvolk office.

"Help," announced Karl when he spotted Harold. "We have some clothing certificates but no idea where to locate the merchandise."

Harold was only too happy to help. He thought that this was an opportunity for him to learn about the functioning of this office.

"Let me have these papers." He had seen many entitlements for entities like a hospital but never for individuals.

"Sit down for a moment, I'll be right back."

Karl looked around the small room which featured a desk and some shelving on the back wall. There was not a single chair in sight. The boys sat on the desk watching a female technician from the phone company installing some equipment on the wall. Neither Karl's nor Peter's parents nor relatives owned a phone. They observed with interest how the woman made some test calls. She smiled at the boys.

"It's all yours and ready to go," she said, then turned to leave.

"Please, hold on for a moment," Karl jumped from the desk and looked at the phone. "Am I able to call with this anyone I wish with this line or is this just a line to the HJ Headquarters?"

"You can call anyone in this country," answered the technician.

"Who pays for the call?" Peter wanted to know.

"The NSDAP (Nazi party) will be billed for it." She pointed to a printed guideline she had place on the desk. "Just read the instruction manual. It will tell you what you are allowed to do." She was halfway out of the door when she turned around. "Let me show you how to place a call. Whom do you wish to call?" She looked expectantly at the boys, ready to help.

Karl twisted his upper body before he found an answer. "I don't know anybody who owns a phone. Do you know someone?" he asked of Peter.

"No, I don't either."

"Well, good luck with it." The woman smiled once more at the boys before she left.

"This lady must be old, did you noticed that she had gray hair?" Karl, always observant, asked his friend. "Of course I saw that. My father says that it is a terrible shame that this war causes women to work." Peter voiced his father's opinion.

"My grandfather says the same thing. He says that a woman should be placed on a pedestal but never allowed to work," Karl agreed.

"What does he mean, placed on a pedestal?" In Peter's mind was a woman standing on a base, like a statue.

"I really don't know what that means. But, my father told me that when I grow up I should only get married if I can afford a wife. If he ever finds out that my wife is working, I don't have to bother to come home anymore. His door would be closed. He meant it too."

Karl loved his father and in spite of his harsh rules he was determined to live up to them. He could not imagine that his mother would have to work. But he was feeling uneasy thinking about his future. The war made it seem impossible to plan for a specific career. He wondered if he could ever afford a wife.

He was glad when Harold entered to chase the 'grown up' thoughts from his mind.

The constantly grinning boy had still the certificates in his hand. "This will be an interesting trial run. If we play our cards right you will not only get your stuff but you might not even have to pay for it." He placed another printed form in front of the boys. "Just fill in the shoe sizes and leave all the other lines open. I will take care of it when I get a typewriter tomorrow morning."

"When did you learn how to type?" wondered Karl.

"Oh, there was a side course in the Napola, about three months ago. I took it to make the most out of the school program. I asked my father about it and he encouraged me. I think he somehow envisioned this position for me."

The boys filled in the required measurements and handed the papers back to Harold.

"Come back tomorrow afternoon and I might have something for you." Harold stuffed all the forms in a large brown envelope. It looked like he intended to take it home in the evening.

Karl would have liked a faster answer but he trusted his friend's ability. He knew that Harold would take this up with his father and so far this had always produced some amazing results.

"What else did you study or learn while you were at the Napola?" Peter was keen to hear additional details from Harold. He had also, a year ago, applied to the cadet school and like Karl he had been rejected.

"Well, we had a few choices besides languages. So I picked basic introduction to economics. However, after the first few sessions I dropped out of it. As an excuse I claimed that I was overwhelmed with the English vocabulary."

"What was your real reason?" Karl was curious.

"The beginning of the course was harmless enough and even interesting, but then they changed instructors on us."

"And?" Karl pressed.

"To make it short, it was more like an introduction to the Nazi belief system than an economics class. We were told that the dismal economic condition of the twenties was a result of Jewish merchants, traders and bankers."

"I heard the same gospel from some of our teachers in Stralau." Peter interjected. "We had a very strict female instructor who did not tolerate any questions," he added.

Karl was thinking in a different direction. "Alright, let's for a moment take the propaganda away from it. What was it that you found interesting in the beginning of the course?"

Harold had to think to remember. "I found the rules governing the interest rates interesting. We were told that since biblical times the cost of money was always three percent per annum, plus the local inflation rate."

Karl did some fast calculations in his head. "Then we should have an interest rate of 8 percent. Figuring present inflation rate at 5 percent."

He shook his head. "How come our interest rate is higher?"

"You are correct," answered Peter. "Taking your figures as valid, we call everything above 8 percent excessive."

Karl was back to the fault heaped on the Jewish bankers.

"I understand that the present interest rate has something to do with the costs of the present war. But I might be wrong. What I don't understand is why the hyperinflation of 1922 and 1923 is being blamed on the Jews."

"You hit the nail on the head," exclaimed Harold. "I felt we were being misled for some kind of a propaganda purpose. They did not teach us any facts except that the money was actually called 'Jew confetti'. This is exactly why I discontinued the class."

Peter was fascinated by what he heard. "We did not learn too much about hyperinflation in our school. Or maybe I was sick or something. I don't remember. Did your teachers mention any figures?" He hoped to get some answers from Harold.

"No, we did not cover this in our school either. What little I know I was told by my grandfather who lived through these times. He told me that in the height of the inflation, I think it was in the month of June in 1923, the price of one liter of milk increased from 1,800 Marks to 3,700 Marks and the price of one egg went from 800 Marks to 2,200 Marks. The price shot up every day."

"These prices are mind boggling. How could the wages keep up with it," contemplated Peter. "It sounds as if the purchase power was gone within a few days."

"Exactly, this is why not only the workers, but every salaried person demanded to be paid on a daily basis," Karl elaborated.

"Did your granddad tell you anymore about it?" Peter seemed more than just mildly interested.

"Not that I remember, but he gave me some history books that I kept. I will bring you one or two along and you are welcome to read them in camp."

"If you have any more books on this subject I'd like to read them too." Harold was just as eager as Peter.

"I might," Karl was not sure. "But there must be some around in the old book stores. Maybe they will allow you to borrow them."

"No, Karl, I think the Nazi's have pulled them off the shelves. I wanted to read up on it and could not find a single one."

"Makes perfect sense," retorted Karl. "Why confuse someone with facts when you have a readymade scapegoat."

For a moment it seemed that his remark went over Peter's head but then he caught himself. "Got it."

While the boys were involved in their discussion they didn't notice that an older HJ member had been listening to them.

"Then I take that you think that the Jews were not responsible," he challenged and looked directly at Karl. He was a bit oversized for his age and seemed to be self-impressed.

"Not so," answered Karl evenly. "I just stated that our schools did not teach us about these times and Harold here mentioned that there are no books on this subject available. So how can I think about something I know nothing about?"

He did not succeed in putting the tough guy on the defensive.

"Never mind your glib answer. You better be careful with your fancy words. I will be watching you." He stretched his body to his full height.

Karl just smiled at him. Putting bullies in their place was what he liked, so he changed his approach.

"I will be very mindful of what I say. Thank you for the warning." He smiled some more at the big boy. "You must be close to eighteen years old, so I am sure that you know what you are talking about. I'll be happy to learn from you." The large fellow was obviously pleased to have Karl succumb.

"No, I am not eighteen years old, I am barely seventeen, but I would be happy to teach you what I know. It is just too bad that I will be drafted in a few days."

"This is great, congratulations," beamed Karl. "This will give you an excellent chance to defend your opinion. I am happy for you." He turned on his heel and left the big boy wondering about the answer.

The air raid sirens wailed just as the boys wanted to leave for home. In accordance with the standing orders, they had to seek immediate shelter. They started to head for the public air raid shelter located in the neighboring school building when the first bombs detonated. They sounded awfully close to them and the whole building seemed to shake. The bombs were hitting before the last sound of the sirens subsided. There must have been some glitch with the early warning system. Even the flak was late in opening up. But even so, within less than thirty seconds the sidewalk connecting the office building with the school was being peppered with shrapnel from the exploding anti-aircraft shells.

"Stop," said the seventeen year old. He was standing between Karl and Peter, who wanted to dash out of the door. "It would be suicidal trying to reach the school." He turned to face Harold who was standing behind him. "Where is the entrance to the basement of this building?"

Harold looked around, searching to find the white arrow with the big letters 'Schutzraum' (shelter) stenciled above it. According to wartime law, every street entrance to a building had to display clearly marked directions to the basement.

"Over here!" Peter had found the entrance and was on his way down. The cellar consisted of a long hallway with small, maybe eight-foot by eight-foot cubicles on each side.

Originally every one of the tenants was entitled to his own cubicle to store coals and winter potatoes and maybe some personal belongings like a bicycle. The units used to have wooden doors with padlocks to prevent pilfering from neighbors but now there was nothing to hoard. The wooden doors had all been burned in the coal ovens of the apartments.

Almost every one of the stalls now featured wooden benches and sometimes a folding bed. Whenever the alarm sounded, the tenants carried bedding and blankets along with their emergency suitcases down to the cellar. It was much harder on the way up, after the all-clear signal sounded. You could not leave anything unattended. Nobody trusted anyone. Too many people had been arrested and disappeared without a trace. Even some of the old-time tenants, who had lived for half a lifetime next door to each other, did not talk to each other anymore.

The fear that someone would steal a blanket or a pillow was made worse by the fact that all the basements served as public shelter and had to be kept unlocked by law.

NINETEEN

Peter found several stalls which were clearly marked 'HJ shelter.' There was not a single folding bed in any of them but plenty of old wooden boxes to sit on. The units must have belonged to some former office tenant because there was no old coal dust on the somewhat clean floor. The noise of the nearby detonating bombs resonated throughout the basement, drowning out the mumble of the shelter seeking tenants. Karl hoped to find a box next to a wall so he could rest his back against it when he saw Peter staring at the floor. Karl followed Peter's gaze and noticed water all over the floor. It was hard to determine where it came from but it was definitely rising. Not very fast but steadily creeping up.

Other people had seen it too and started to move towards the single exit door. It caused some confusion until the tenants still coming down the cellar stairs understood what was going on.

Karl was amazed at the discipline displayed under these trying circumstances. There were some senior HJ members who took control of the situation by racing up to the street level entrance to stop anyone from entering the staircase. While the evacuation of the basement was relatively swift and orderly, it gave way to a mixed state of affairs in the main hallway. Nobody knew where to seek safety and it was the HJ again who established some resemblance of order.

The original rain of shrapnel had dissipated as the flak was seeking to engage the bombers over a different district of Berlin. Karl and Harold were ordered to ascertain the condition of the shelter underneath the school building. There was no water in the basement and because it was evening, there were no students around so the shelter was almost empty. Before the second wave of bombers unloaded their freight all the people from the apartment building were safely channeled to the cellar underneath the school.

The air raid lasted over six hours. It was one of the longest Karl had witnessed. Of course his practical experience had been limited by the fact that during the last year he had been mostly away from the city.

By the time he finally reached his home it was past 4:00 AM. Karl was relieved to find his parents safe and sound and they were just as happy to see him.

"Where have you been?" asked his father. "The all clear sounded before 2:00 AM and we were deeply worried."

"I was ordered to help some families with their small children." Karl had hurried home right after he was dismissed by his unit.

"This should not have taken over two hours." Herr Veth was relieved to see his son but he was still upset by his apparent tardiness.

"There was more to it than just simple helping. I had to search with Harold and a few other members through several flooded basements to help find some babies who supposedly were missing." Karl was dripping wet and cold. He wanted nothing more than to get out of his uniform and crawl under his warm feather bedding. But he understood that his parents had been worried.

"Did you find the babies?" His mother handed him two towels and shoved him towards the bathroom.

"No, I think that the mothers or the relatives had been separated in all the confusion. It was a lot of crying and a mess until everything was sorted out. I am really sorry that I worried you."

Karl's mother checked Karl's wet clothing. "They should give you a medal for your effort."

"No, neither Harold nor I got even a thank you when we got out of the last basement. But it was not as bad as it could have been," he added, "just one block over they suffered a busted gas line. They told us that there were over sixty casualties."

"Sixty casualties!" exclaimed his mother. "Was it a direct hit at the shelter?"

"I don't think so. The fireman who walked with us through the basements said something about a 'silent' gas leak which killed without warning. I told you it was a mess. Goodnight."

He did not hear an answer. He was asleep as his head hit the pillow.

The next morning was a little unusual. Karl's father had been permitted to take a day off from work and decided to visit his parents. Karl was allowed to go with his dad to see his granddad once more before his trip to the Harz Mountains.

"Did you hear that Dr. Foster got arrested?" Grandpa Veth asked his son. Karl's father looked up in surprise.

"Dr. Foster? He was the only reliable physician in the neighborhood. Do you know any details?" Dr. Foster had his office in the front building of the apartment complex while the grandparent's apartment was in the rear building. He was a well-known family doctor.

Like all physicians in Berlin, he had his office in his apartment. Medical centers were unknown at that time and if they did exist they would not have been visited. Nobody would have dreamed of visiting a doctor without knowing about his wife, his children and his family life. Besides, people wanted to know where and in which neighborhood their doctor lived. The physicians who served in the hospitals were an exception to this rule.

"The paper only stated that he was arrested. But I heard from our neighbors that he was detained because of unprofessional conduct. Supposedly he was seeing a patient wearing a regular suit." The grandfather summed up what he knew about this incident.

"That will do it." Karl's father turned to his son. "Didn't you just tell me the other day that there are now guidelines published by the propaganda people?"

"Yes, we did receive a 'reporting guideline' which included unprofessional and suspicious behavior," Karl remembered.

"Did they give you any reasons why the propaganda agency issued these rules to the HJ?" Karl's grandfather wondered.

Karl hesitated answering because the instructions had been marked confidential. He also knew that they would upset his Opa. Unsure how to answer he looked to his father for guidance.

"Go ahead and tell Opa what you told me." Herr Veth encouraged his son.

"No, they gave us no specific reasons." Karl wanted to keep this topic short. He did not like the idea of telling on each other and hoped that his reply would suffice.

Herr Veth turned to his father. "It looks to me that Dr. Goebbels' propaganda agency is using the HJ to encourage spying on our citizens. The boys are to report on 'unprofessional conduct' to flush out dissidents of the Nazi doctrine."

"What does Dr. Foster's arrest have to do with this?" pondered the old cavalry officer.

"It fits. A doctor practicing medicine while wearing street clothing is clearly a follower of sloppy, unprofessional bearing," Herr Veth explained.

"Yes, a physician is supposed to wear a white garment when he is seeing a patient," Karl said, opening up. His sense of order agreed with this specific part of the ruling. It was the reporting which bothered him.

"But this cannot be a reason to arrest someone," objected the granddad.

"It is reason enough for the SS to detain anyone who steps out of line. In their mind all professionals who are excused of active duty are nothing but military dodgers. Besides they are not just taken into custody. They are detained in labor camps until they are 'cured' of their transgressions," Karl's father elaborated.

"Yes, I heard about that and I am worried. Grandmother is not doing too well. She was seeing Dr. Foster before the holidays and now she will need to visit a different physician."

While the grownups continued their conversation Karl went to the kitchen to see his grandma. She seemed to be in a good mood and when he asked her about her illness she just shook her grey head.

"Nothing, serious, Karlchen, it will pass. There is always something not working right when you get older. It's either that or you have to die young." She was always cheerful when she spoke to Karl and he was happy to see that she was her usual self.

He went back to the living room and asked to be excused. Today did not seem to be the day to bother his granddad with questions and he wanted to meet with Harold and Peter. He reached the office building just in time to see the fire trucks leaving. They had pumped the basement dry and the building seemed to be back to normal.

"What caused the flooding?" he asked Harold instead of a greeting.

"Some unfortunate devastating hit up the street caused the mainline to rupture and it flooded the neighboring basements. The school shelter was not connected, so it stayed dry."

He reached for a paper on the shelf behind his desk. "Here is the address of a supply depot which stores shoes in your size and here is a cash equivalent certificate for government employees. You will not have to pay for the shoes or the pants."

"I am not a government employee," Karl objected, but he was

surprised at the speed with which Harold had produced the needed address.

"It does not matter, my friend," Harold assured him. "By the time Peter gets here I will have an assignment typed out and stamped by the administrator of this office."

"Who is the administrator of this office?" wondered Karl. "And how will you obtain his signature?"

"Karl, you better get back to your camps. You have been out of touch way too long. You are much too slow for the Berlin of today." Harold reached into his desk drawer and produced several rubber stamps.

"You wouldn't dare, "Karl stammered.

"What?" Harold said, smiling. "First of all there is no real administrator of this office. But I have some stamps who say otherwise. So, I don't need to obtain any particular signature."

He started typing as if he was trying to break a record. Karl was mildly bewildered. Maybe his friend was right and he had been away too long.

Harold finished at about the same time Peter entered the office. He was out of uniform because he had slept at a nearby relative's house. The clothes he was wearing did not exactly fit him but they were clean and dry.

"How good are you with signing with your left hand?" Harold greeted him. Peter did not know what to make with the question. He had no experience in signing anything. Right or left handed. He pushed both of his fists in his pockets and just stood there with his silly grin on his face.

Harold was not perturbed. He opened the door and waved at an old looking street worker who was busy brushing the last debris from the sidewalk. "Do you smoke?" he inquired.

"Of course, who doesn't?" answered the old guy. Harold grabbed the papers and again reached into his desk drawer. He shook two cigarettes out of a packet and went outside. A moment later he was back and pressed his rubber stamp over signatures that nobody could read. He had to give both papers to Karl because Peter refused to take his hands out of his pockets.

Two hours later the boys were back. Both had a pair of brand new leather shoes in a paper bag and Karl also had two pairs of uniform pants.

"You were right," marveled Karl. "They never asked for money or anything." He was elated.

"Interesting," muttered Harold. "I'll be darned. This was my first attempt and it seems to work. I have to remember what I did."

He pushed the desk clean of some scattered papers and unfolded a railroad and subway map of the city. "Remember the footpath you found?" he asked Karl. "I had some time to go back and found that the grate was unlocked. The grate and the culvert was nothing but a decoy. The path opened up again and ended right under a dead, unused track of rails." He touched a specific point on the map. Karl could see that it was fairly close to the long distance railroad platform at the Zoo Station.

"How was the exit concealed?" Karl admired that his friend had pursued their exploration.

"Just a simple grate among the lose Schotter (railroad rocks). There was a thin layer on top of the grate but otherwise it was right in the open." Harold pushed the map closer to Karl who leaned over the desk. "What do you make of it?" he asked.

"I am not sure, but it looks like an escape or infiltration route," Karl guessed.

Harold thumbed the map a few times." There is no question that this is an escape tunnel. Nobody in his right mind would infiltrate the subway system. What for? Another thing, it is clear that the tunnel is old, but it is still in active use. What we don't know is who is using it."

Peter had listened to the friends and wondered about their exploits. His eyes went from the map to the boys and back. "What do you intend to do with this information?" he asked.

Karl had nothing to say and looked at Harold. "We could report it to the SS," said Harold, uncertain of the possible consequences.

"No, I don't like that. Whoever is using it, is just trying to get out of Berlin. That's all." Karl wished he had never discovered the trail. "Why don't we stay away from this subway section and simply forget about it. After all, it is none of our business. Besides Peter and I will be gone anyhow," he suggested.

"I agree, we can always 'remember' the path when it suits us." Harold looked like he was relieved. "Will I see you once more before you leave?" he asked, looking hopefully at Karl.

"Don't know about that," Karl said, stretching out his hand. "First of all, thank you, but now that you have a phone why don't you give me your number? I should be able to use the camp phone. It would be nice to stay in contact."

Harold searched the phone instruction sheet to find it and then noticed that it was written on a small piece of paper and taped below the dial. It was a six-digit number starting with 92. No prefix.

"You did a great job with getting us our shoes. Thank you." Peter shook Harold's hand. He was eager to get to his parents in Stralau. "See you next week at the railroad station," he waved at Karl.

A day later Karl saw his grandfather again. He told him about the subway path because he wanted to hear his granddad's take on it. "Do you think that it could be an escape tunnel for Jews?" he asked him.

"It might have been in 1938 or in 39. But Harold thinks that it is still active?"

"Yes, that's what he said."

"You did right by deciding to forget about it. I would not be surprised if the SS is using it to smuggle valuables out of Berlin. They have been secretly plundering some of our museums under the pretext of storing the artifacts in underground shelters."

Karl considered the possibility. "I cannot imagine that the SS is doing anything in secret. They are all over the place and can ship out whatever they please."

"Yes," agreed Karl's grandfather, "but you are talking about the organized units. I am thinking more of individual officers who have access and opportunities. The smart ones know that we will lose the war and they are hording right now." He looked for his walking stick and reached for a cap. "You better go home. I have some errands to take care of." He was curious about Karl's little story and wanted to visit his friend, the switch master. He should know what kind of trains are routinely parked above the possible exit grate.

A week later Karl was in the Harz Mountains. By now he had enough experience with his assignment that it took him very little time to establish a routine with Peter. In essence it was always the same. Peter took care of the sport programs and Karl initiated little work details.

The camp was located in Allrode and Thale, two little villages featuring houses with incredibly steep roof lines. Karl had never seen anything like it. Most of the houses were of the Fachwerk (half timbered) construction and it inspired him to order assorted painting supplies from Berlin for the boys. He then proceeded to guide small groups of 10 or 12 boys to different locations and all of them competed to draw and paint on writing paper various likenesses of the pretty houses. After the teachers graded the artwork (all of them achieved at least a C grading), the boys sent the pictures home. It was unfortunate that none of the teachers were art teachers.

However, one of the women teachers was versed in the history of the area and took groups of boys to the many locations of the fairy tales the brothers Grimm had written about. They also visited the nearby Wartburg castle in which Martin Luther had translated the Bible into German. According to history it was here that Martin Luther had thrown an inkwell at the devil.

"Now, that story is a stretch," Peter muttered to Karl when they looked at the stain on the wall. It was in a small cubicle and the supposedly original writing utensils were displayed on a small writing desk. The teacher as well as the castle guide, a woman Karl estimated to be in her seventies, insisted that it was an ink stain. "Alright, maybe it is a true ink stain." Peter allowed. "But, the thing with the devil is a bit much."

He was not born yesterday, he explained to Karl, who was more open-minded.

"Maybe the devil was something of a vision," he opinioned to Peter.

"You are nuts, there is no such thing as a vision. The Martin fellow, or whatever his name is, was besoffen (drunk), that's when you get visions. My father told me so. This is the reason that I will never touch an alcoholic drink." To the horror of the castle guide he proclaimed his view loudly to the boys in the room. It was the only time that Karl had to pull rank on him to shut him up.

TWENTY

Karl and Peter spent three months at the camp before they were ordered back to Berlin. Their new assignment was a camp in Poland. It was an old cloister located close to the small town of Kosten. This time there were not even woman teachers available. The boys were told that it would be a smaller camp, maybe not more than 120 boys, again between ages eight and ten.

Their new camp leader was supposed to be a Lieutenant. A former panzer commander who had been heavily wounded and had suffered two amputations. When the boys reported to their first meeting with the KLV officials, the officer was not present. Apparently he was still recuperating in a field hospital.

When Karl told his grandfather of his new assignment the old officer was stunned. "Kosten, in Poland? How can the KLV administration be so shortsighted? You will be overrun by the Russians. I don't even think that the whole war will last more than a year. Do whatever you can to get out of this task." He was clearly upset.

Karl's father didn't like it any better. "Of all the safe places in Germany, what are they thinking to establish a new camp in Poland?"

Even Peter's mother was worried. Peter's father served someplace in Russia and the Feldpost- military postal service- was sometimes delayed by weeks. She feared that she might not be able to stay in touch with her son.

"What do we do?" asked Peter when he saw Karl a few days later.

"I don't know," admitted Karl. "I don't believe that we have a choice in this matter. However, I will talk with Harold. It would not surprise me if he has an inside line to the KLV."

It turned out to be the opposite. While Harold had connections, mostly through his father, to all kind of goodies, it was Karl who was solidly established with the school administration. He went to see Herr Hartung to ask him if there was a choice of destinations.

"No, Karl, I don't know how to tell you, but it seems you did too well of a job. All of our present camps run smoothly and your assignment to Kosten is actually recognition of your efforts." The administrator rolled his chair from behind the desk. He wanted the meeting to be informal because he liked the boy.

Karl wondered if he missed something. Maybe he was just slow this morning. "I am not so sure that I deserve a prize, but I don't understand how a camp in Poland is a reward." He wanted to add that his parents thought that Poland was possibly the worst place, but his respect for the invalid hindered him from rattling on.

"No, Karl, you misunderstand. It is not the destination, it is the camp itself which is an acknowledgement of your leadership abilities." He gestured to Karl to sit down. "I understand that you are worried about the Russians and that is understandable, but let me explain. The leader of this camp in Kosten will be a severely handicapped officer who has some teaching abilities. You and Peter will not only be his assistants but you will be empowered to take control of the camp in case something happens to the officer."

Herr Hartung debated with himself how much he should tell Karl about the gravity of the situation.

The male teachers had been drafted and the few remaining female teachers in Berlin were not volunteering for a camp so close to the Russian lines. The school administration was forced to issue stern orders with the result that the teachers simply did not show up. The 'blue' letters which had been sent out came back with the remark 'moved, not at this address.' Sometimes the letters came back "bombed out. No forwarding address.' In any event it was the same. No teachers for KLV camp duty.

"Of course neither you nor Peter will be expected to teach, but you both have shown that you are able to maintain sanitary conditions and keep the students occupied. You will be rewarded with promotions." He saw that the boy was squirming in his chair. "But this is not all. You will stay in constant contact with us and we will render any assistance you require."

Karl recognized that the Berlin school system was slowly disintegrating. He had seen it coming during the past year. Every time he came back from a camp there was someone new in charge. Mostly a totally clueless official with absolutely no practical experience. Herr Hartung had been the only one who lasted over a year in the position of KLV administrator. He was responsible for all the school districts in Berlin. All the other bureaucrats were nothing but replacements for replacements.

"But why Poland? I have seen several places in Bavaria and elsewhere that seem to be a lot safer from the Russians," Karl could not help himself. He had to ask.

Herr Hartung had a helpless expression on his face. "I don't know, Karl. I just follow orders."

Karl could feel that he was not getting anywhere. If the head of the KLV system had to follow orders, who was he to question the wisdom of the decision makers.

He got up and saluted the administrator, who waved him off. "One more thing, Karl. You don't need to write any more reports, but I expect you to see me every few weeks and to report to me personally. I will issue you free transportation vouchers to use the railroad whenever you deem it necessary. Check in with me before you leave."

In a way Karl was glad to leave the office. He instinctually liked order and discipline but in the KLV system, both seemed to be unraveling.

"Kosten it is," he announced when he came home. His mother smiled when he told her about the meeting with Herr Hartung.

"I am sure that the NSDAP (Nazi) leadership knows what they are doing. They would not send you to Poland if they thought that there is any chance the camp could be overrun by the Russians. Don't forget that Herr Hitler is in charge, and don't forget his wonder weapons."

Karl's father however, did not seem to share her sentiment. He was worried about his son.

The transport to Kosten left a week later and Karl met his new camp leader for the first time. His name was Lothar Hardfeld. He was in the black uniform of a panzer commander and carried the rank of a lieutenant. His right hand was missing and so was the foot and lower part of his right leg. Karl guessed his age to be in the late forties. Karl hit it off with him from the moment he saw him.

"My name is Karl Veth. I am your sub leader. Please leave the boarding of the students to Peter Zahn, your other sub leader and to me. We are versed in the procedure," he snapped his sharpest salute and the lieutenant was visibly pleased.

"I heard about you, Karl, and I am glad that you are assigned to my camp."

It was shortly after 8:00 AM and after the usual ceremonies the train left nearly on time. It would have been only a four hour trip but troop carrier trains forced the children transport to stop several times at small railroad stations to let the military trains pass.

Karl had studied the map of the Kosten area and he was prepared for a one hour march from the railroad station to the cloister. He was wondering how the lieutenant could do this with his prosthesis. To his surprise there were several horse-drawn farm wagons waiting for them at the station. Peter arranged for the backpacks and suitcases to be loaded and helped Lieutenant Hardfeld to climb on the first wagon. Karl was a little concerned when he saw that some of the students were barely 8 years old. It was a cool April evening and he did not know what the condition at the cloister was like. He hoped that the building had a warm hall or at least some wood stoves in the sleeping arrangements.

But first things first. He made sure that all of the youngest children had a seat on the wagon and then divided the remainder of the children in two groups. They would alternately march for fifteen minutes and then ride on the wagons. The lieutenant kept time because neither Karl nor Peter owned a watch.

The cloister turned out to be much more comfortable than Karl had anticipated. While it was a very old building - Karl had heard something about it being 200 years old - it featured large fireplaces and there was plenty of birch wood stacked under rainproof covers.

The boys were greeted by three polish women who introduced themselves in passable German. They were cooks and general care takers. They had the main hall very well heated and served a nice hot vegetable soup to the children.

Karl and Peter inspected the sleeping quarters. They were rather primitive compared to the previous camps where they had stayed. There was no real bedding, but plenty of straw-filled feed bags. To make it worse only a few of the sleeping rooms featured fireplaces and all of them were stone cold.

"Well, this is most certainly a disappointment. Any suggestions?" They could hear the voice from the lieutenant who had followed them. Peter looked at Karl to come up with something

"We will make a game of it. We let the boys drag the straw bags out of the cubicles and show them how to make their own sleeping arrangements in the main hall. The ones who settle down the fastest will be awarded their choice of rooms tomorrow morning."

"Sounds good to me," agreed the lieutenant. "We will set a time limit. The ones who are not bedded down within an hour will have to sleep in a cold room. At least this is what we will tell them," he added.

Peter looked expectantly at Karl. "You are the one in charge of hygiene. I have not seen a single wash room and only a few dry toilets. How are you going to handle this?"

"Easy," said Karl. "We will show them the location of the toilets and tell them that they don't need to wash themselves until tomorrow when we will have this building sorted out. The kids will love it."

He was right. The students thought that their sub leader was a great guy to let them go to sleep without washing up and within an hour after the meal everyone had found a place to sleep.

Everyone, except the lieutenant. He had taken a notion from Karl's previous arrangement and had helped to get the youngest ones to sleep closest to the large fireplace. "Now what?" his face showed that he was in pain as he babied his right arm.

"Call me mother," mumbled Karl to himself and searched for the Polish women. He found them were he suspected they would be; in the huge kitchen. After a few questions he was informed that there were two additional rooms next to the kitchen and actually right behind the big dining hall. They were pleasantly heated from the stone wall which separated them from the main fireplace. The cooks occupied one of the rooms but the other one would be suitable for the lieutenant. There was however a huge drawback. The nearest toilet was on the far side of the dining hall.

"Thank you Karl. I am more than happy to take this room." Lieutenant Hardfeld did not seem to mind at all.

The next few days were filled with getting the camp organized.

Karl discovered that there were plenty of wash rooms. They were in a separate building that featured rather large storage tanks to prevent the water from freezing. There was also a boiler room and the lieutenant and Peter created a makeshift warm-water system.

Karl noticed on the second day that one of the younger boys nursed a heavily bandaged left hand. His name was Bernd and when Karl called him to join him in the kitchen he wanted to hide his hand behind his back.

"Let me see what's bothering you."

"Nothing," answered Bernd.

"Then why is your hand covered?" Karl reached for boy's hand.

Bernd flinched at first but then allowed Karl to remove the bandage. There was no open wound but the whole hand was swollen to nearly twice the normal size. The knuckles were blue and red and Bernd was unable to move his fingers except for his thumb.

"You are left handed, Bernd?" Karl asked the boy.

The boy hesitated before he answered. "Yes." Karl noted the fearful expression in Bernd's face.

"You don't have to worry any more. Please tell me who did this to you."

"Nobody." Bernd was almost shaking in fear of being beaten again on his hand, but something in Karl's voice told him that he could trust him.

"You got hit with a stick, didn't you?"

Bernd nodded, holding back his tears.

"Who hit you? A teacher or other children?" Karl wanted to ascertain if the boy had been punished by his class mates.

Bernd did not answer, his eyes pleaded with Karl to stop questioning him. But Karl had to know. There was a hard stigma against left-handed children and if the injury was caused by other children he had to separate the boy from the group who did this to him.

"Bernd, look at me. In this camp I am your friend. You have nothing to fear and I want to help you. You don't have to answer. Just nod or shake your head when I ask you something. Will you do this?"

Bernd nodded.

Karl looked once more at the information tag that dangled from Bernd's neck.

"Are you nine years old?"

Bernd nodded his head.

"Has a teacher hit you on this hand before?"

Another nod from Bernd.

"Did any classmates ever hit you?"

A vigorous shaking of Bernd's head confirmed Karl's guess that the injury was caused by a teacher. Every student who was left-handed was automatically considered an idiot or at least a dummy who could only be cured by severe beatings on the left hand. If he would learn to write and work with his right (the correct) hand he was considered to be healed. If not, it was considered to be proof that he was indeed a dummy. This was the common belief in Germany in the 1940s. Employment for a left-handed person was nearly impossible to obtain. Who wanted to employ someone who did not know how to use the correct hand?

The teachers did their best to ensure that their students grew up to be employable and routinely disciplined the left-handers. Most of the time they were called to the front of the class. They were then shown several sticks and permitted to select the one which was then used to punish them.

Some of the teachers were more lenient and did not hurt the boys. They just bandaged the hand so that the student could not use it. Karl had noticed that the left-handed girls never got 'corrected' and had asked his granddad about it.

"You don't need to teach a person who will never seek employment. A girl will grow up to be a woman and women shall not work other than to take care of her children and her husband."

This conversation happened over two years ago and his granddad summed it up in two sentences.

Karl realized that he had a little challenge on his hand. He didn't know the lieutenant's take on left handers but one thing was for sure, as long as he was in this camp nobody would touch Bernd. He took the boy by his right hand and went looking for Hardfeld. He found him tending to the boiler in the wash room building and decided on a direct approach.

"Look at Bernd's hand, please, Herr Lieutenant."

Hardfeld examined the hand. "This is not as bad as it looks. Nothing is broken. Unfortunately we cannot bring charges against the teacher who did this, but, thanks for bringing this to my attention."

Karl was glad to hear that the camp leader, who seemed to be in constant pain, was on his side. He decided to ask Harold for some pain medication when he was in Berlin again.

He was taking Bernd back to his friends when he heard loud shouting from the camp gate. Peter had initiated a simple guard detail which patrolled the entry to the camp. In practicality it was unnecessary, but it made the older boys feel important and it gave them something to write home about it.

"Jesus imitator is coming, Jesus imitator is coming!" The

shouting got louder as more boys joined in. When Karl got to the gate he was joined by Peter who had also heard the commotion.

Indeed, there was a man passing in front of the gate wearing sandals. There was no beach for hundreds of miles around where sandals might have been condoned as acceptable footwear. But here, in the middle of the country? There was no doubt in the minds of the children that this fellow was imitating Jesus. Every one of them had heard at one time or another about this ancient fellow who about two thousand years ago had traveled through the desert wearing sandals. Anyone wearing sandals now, in 1944, was called a Jesus Ersatz, or imitator.

In 1938 and 1939 the SS had a field day hunting down people wearing sandals. Hundreds if not thousands had been arrested and wound up in concentration camps. It was proclaimed that anyone wearing sandals was either a HungAryan tramp, a Jew or a German drifter sympathizing with the undesirables.

Karl was perplexed about the audacity of the stranger. He could not remember when he had seen an adult wearing this kind of footwear.

"Come over here," he waved at the passerby. The man, who seemed to be in his thirties, glanced at Karl's uniform and for a moment it looked as if he wanted to run away. He probably would have if it hadn't been for Wanda, one of the Polish camp cooks. She had joined the hubbub at the gateway and was now calling out to the man in Polish.

"He is a Polish farmhand on the way home," she explained to Karl.

"Ask him if he knows that sandals might get him arrested." Karl knew that anyone of the boys could report him if he did not challenge the stranger.

"Yes, he knows. But this is the only footwear he owns and he apologizes if he offended you," Wanda translated.

Karl studied the field worker and felt sorry for him. It was obvious that the man was frightened by Karl's uniform. He glowered repeatedly at the lieutenant who had now also joined the ruckus.

"Ask him if he is hungry." Karl decided to use this incident to possibly gain a friend in this otherwise hostile country.

"Yes," confirmed Wanda, "they feed him only one meal per day."

Karl conferred for a moment with Hardfeld and then turned to the boys. "This is a poor Polish worker who does not own a pair of shoes. He wears sandals because this is all he has. He is not to be confused with a German Jesus imitator. We will feed the stranger because he is hungry."

"Peter, please take the boys inside. I want to talk to them after I am done." He turned to Wanda. "You understand that I cannot invite him to join us. So please, give him something to eat and tell him that he has nothing to fear from us." He walked up to the chap to shake his hand.

The guy did not know what to think of Karl and extended his hand very slowly but then grinned when he heard Wanda's translation.

"Well done, Karl. We have uncertain times ahead of us. I like what you did." The lieutenant followed Karl's example and shook the stranger's hand.

Karl did not look back or check in any way what kind of food Wanda was serving the field hand. He felt pretty sure that she would not overstep her position.

"Already covering your behind? We have hardly arrived." Peter was grinning from ear to ear.

"No, Peter, I was not covering my behind. My behind was not on the line. I was merely trying to establish good will." Karl conveyed the same message to the boys in the dining hall. "Whenever you meet a Polish resident, I expect you to be polite. Not more and surely not less." He concluded his short speech.

A few weeks later he was in Berlin and reported to administrator Hartung about the incident. Hartung assured him that he had done the correct thing. "You are turning fourteen within a few weeks and you have to join the Hitler Youth. I had a request from the HJ headquarters to release you from your position. You are supposed to undergo regular infantry training."

He expected Karl to say something. A minute passed and Karl waited patiently for the remainder of the bad news. But, it was far better than he had expected.

"I intervened on your behalf and also because I need you in Kosten. You will only have to undergo a crash course as a sniper."

He fumbled with the papers on his desk. "I arranged for you to be trained by a special mentor. He is an officer with a parachute commando and supposed to be the very best instructor currently available." He found what he was looking for and handed Karl an envelope with some instructions.

"Make me proud." Karl was dismissed. He spent the next twelve days at a training facility close to the Tempelhof Airport. At night he was permitted to sleep at home and enjoyed the evenings with his parents and his brother and sister. However the nights were almost always interrupted with air raid alarms and many times he found hardly any sleep at all.

He graduated from his training with the highest points possible. The shooting itself was only part of the training. The other part was spent learning the art of finding cover and how to always have an escape route planned.

On the day he had to return to Kosten his grandma was admitted to a hospital. She died five days later and Karl was granted a special leave to attend her funeral. He was shocked to see how much his Opa had aged. Karl was proud of him as the old cavalry officer stood next to his father for a long time at the grave. He hoped to have a few words with him after the ceremony but the old timer wanted to be left alone and the family respected his wishes.

A few weeks later Karl turned fourteen and was now formally a member of the HJ. Due to the fact that he was a sub leader of a KLV camp he was immediately promoted to Gefolgschaftfuehrer. To his surprise he was also permitted to wear a silver eagle on his cap. This was actually a much higher recognition of his abilities than the promotion. Regular HJ members could only display the HJ emblem on their cap.

"This is highly unusual," remarked Harold when Karl visited him during one of his routine trips to Berlin. "You are barely fourteen years old and I have never seen an eagle on anyone's cap below the age of twenty."

Karl shrugged his shoulders as he always did when he had no answer. "You have to talk to Herr Hartung about this. I think that it was his doing."

"Why would he want to do that?" wondered Harold. "Do I have to salute you now too, or what?"

"Yeah, good idea. But make it snappy. I strongly dislike sloppy salutes."

Harold knew that his friend was only jesting, but never-the-less he was deeply impressed with Karl's uniform and position.

"I almost forgot to tell you, I will be back in a few weeks to attend a driving course for motorcycles," Karl informed his friend.

"Hmm," said Harold, "I am almost afraid to ask, but whose idea is that?"

"Herr Hartung," Karl replied with a smile.

"And may I ask why?"

"He wants me to know how to drive in case the Russians break our lines."

"Well, that takes care of your ability but not of the motor cycle itself. Where do you get that?"

"I was hoping that you could help me with the answer." Karl said with a smile.

"Well, at the very least it will be a challenge," Harold seemed to be optimistic and then added "I wanted to tell you this before; I went last week to our mystery foot path in the subway. It is gone"

"It is gone? It cannot walk, what do you mean it is gone?" Karl wanted to understand.

"No, off course it did not get up and walk away. But, it disappeared. The entrance is totally filled in and it looks like it never existed." Harold was sure of what he had seen.

Two months later Karl attended the driving course and shortly thereafter his little world began to crumble.

He was in the camp when two messages reached him within a short interval of each other.

The first one was from his father informing him that his Opa had been arrested by the SS. No reason was given. One day he was in his apartment and the next day he was gone.

The second message was from his mother. His father had been drafted into the Volkssturm, the final German call to arms. She intended to leave Berlin with his brother and sister to live with a relative in Westphalia (a western state of Germany.)

It was a week before Christmas 1944 when he learned that Herr Hartung had committed suicide. Again, just a short message without any explanation.

Karl realized that he had to rely on himself.

Karl's story continues.
Please turn the page for a preview of:

LOYAL TO A DEGREE
Growing Up Under The Third Reich: Book 2

LOYAL TO A DEGREE

Growing Up Under The Third Reich: Book 2

BASED ON A TRUE STORY

Horst Christian

ONE

1:25 AM

Karl turned the radio off. He had just listened to the German special OKW report, which announced a breakthrough of Russian tanks at a German defense line 180 kilometers east of his camp.

This was the news Karl had anticipated and feared for the last seven days. He knew that he had to act fast if there was any chance left to bring the kids from the KLV camp back to Berlin. His camp was located in a 200-year-old cloister near Kosten in Poland. It had served for the past two years as an evacuation camp for children from Berlin.

The leader of the camp was Lieutenant Lothar Hardfeld, a former tank commander who had lost his right hand and the lower half of his right leg during an explosion of an ammunition depot. After his amputations and partial recovery in a field hospital, he was declared unfit to fight and had been ordered to oversee the "air attack evacuation" camp of school children from Berlin.

Since no teachers were available, he was also ordered to conduct some minimal teaching of the German language and also arithmetic. At 46 years of age he was the only adult in the camp of 122 boys, almost all of them under the age of 12 years.

Karl Veth, his assistant, was a brown haired blue eyed 14-year old. He was short for his age; only 5'3 and he weighed 124 pounds. Because of his physical build, he was trained as a sniper in the German HJ (Hitler Youth). He was in charge of food and personal hygiene.

Karl's best friend was another 14-year old HJ member named Peter Zahn.

Peter was in charge of physical education, which mostly consisted of long distance running and some ball games. However, after the only ball in the camp disappeared, it was only running; every day at least 2 kilometers, which was not much but still a good distance to run for the age group.

After Karl had turned off the radio he looked over to the other bunk bed and noticed that his friend was peacefully sleeping. "Peter," he whispered, and then louder, "Peter, wake up. The Russians broke the line and could be here within 24 hours."

As Peter looked up Karl added, "Run and wake Hardfeld, but don't wait for him to fire any questions at you because I have no further details. Just tell him that the Russians are coming and then ring the alarm for the camp. If he asks for me, just tell him that I am in the bathroom throwing up and that I will meet him at the front entrance."

While Peter fumbled around in the dark to find his uniform, Karl was already out the door and running towards the back of the hallway. The few candles on the walls of the cloister were the only illumination the camp had for the last few weeks, barely enough to keep you from banging into the moist cobblestone walls. But Karl could have found his way anyhow, even in total darkness, and as he approached the last door on the right he quickly entered and closed the door behind him. He did not like the room very much. It was very small, more like a closet and it was currently being used for storage of old broken down snow shovels.

It wasn't the shovels that gave him the creeps; it was more the many rats that scurried around and squeaked when disturbed.

It had been about six weeks back that Karl had found this room by accident when he was on night guard duty. He had followed a weird sound that seemed to emerge from the end of the hallway.

What he found was this closet. It covered an entrance to an underground passageway leading from the main living part of the cloister to the actual chapel. The sound came from people shuffling around and talking to each other.

He discovered Polish people; old people, mostly women and one old priest apparently trying to read mass or something.

Karl did not understand the Polish language, but he knew that this was strange because as far as he knew, the church section of the cloister had been sealed shut a few years ago. The Polish people who tended to the maintenance of the cloister had been forced to leave, and anyhow, church services at this place were not permitted.

As he tried to get a better look at the meeting he somehow locked eyes with the priest who proceeded to read from a book, but a slight movement of his hand told Karl that he had been detected and should stay at his place.

A few moments later the priest stopped reading and announced something that Karl did not understand, but all of the sudden the meeting broke up. There were actually only five women and one more old man besides the priest.

Karl counted them as they lined up behind a frayed but colorful curtain, apparently to enter another dark staircase leading down. The priest stayed behind and looked again in Karl's direction.

"Come on out, I see you and I think that I know you," he said in broken German, "I will not harm you, but I think that we need to talk."

Karl figured that he could easily overpower the frail looking priest and since he was detected already, he might as well find out what was going on here.

"What are you doing here and what do you want," he asked the priest.

The priest replied with a very thin smile forming on his lips, "This is my home and I am praying, and maybe we can help each other. Are you interested?"

"I don't need any help and I can have you arrested for conducting an unlawful meeting." Karl was weak in his response as he was unsure who would be doing the arresting.

"You are right. You don't need my help right now, but maybe soon. Sooner than you might think." The old clergy continued to smile, "Come, sit down over here and I will tell you what I have to offer and you just might wish to kungle."

Karl was stunned. First, that the old guy spoke a reasonable German, and second, that he used the word kungle, because kungle was not really a common word of the German language, but a recently developed slang word meaning the exchange of goods on the black market.

Let's see what the priest has to kungle, he thought to himself and came out from behind the trap door to sit down on a step stool beside the altar.

"What do you have that you think I might need," he asked locking eyes with the priest.

"For one thing," the old man answered, "I have civilian clothes for you and for your friend Peter. You will need them real soon. I might also have underground information you will certainly need to get back to Germany alive."

Karl thought quickly. This guy was right on both counts. Karl's only clothing was his uniform which identified him as a Jungschar leader and a sniper. Of course, he could get rid of all the insignia, but it was still a uniform, and if he ripped off the patches, it would show on the fabric. Also, getting back to Germany alive depended a lot on evading the Polish underground movement.

"You might be right, let's kungle. What do you want in exchange?"

"We need food and medical supplies. I know that you have access to them," the priest answered.

"You seem to know a lot about our present condition and about me. Maybe even too much, and yet I know nothing about you. I did not even know that you or your meetings here existed. And most of all, I don't know if I can trust you."

"You can't trust me, you know that, because you cannot trust anyone anymore, but we need each other and we need to establish what you call trust and what I call a common ground relationship. I show you my goodwill by offering you a pair of used but very well insulated winter shoes. With the shoes you are now wearing you will not get 10 kilometers from here, especially if it is snowing and it will, within a few weeks."

The old man had hit the nail right on the head. Karl had been worrying about his footwear for quite a while. It was badly in need of replacement and there was not even a remote possibility of getting a Bezugsschein, an entitlement form, but even those were by themselves useless.

The stores were empty of merchandise. The only way to obtain anything was by kungling, and shoes, getting them were nearly impossible, unless you knew of a family where someone had died and the family traded off the belongings.

"What do you want for the shoes," Karl asked.

"Soap," the priest answered.

"How do I know that the shoes will fit?"

"Try them on; they are right under the altar." The priest moved a curtain from behind the side altar and pointed to a pile of used but slightly clean looking clothes and a pair of heavy black leather boots.

Karl tried the boots on. They were maybe a size too large but this was perfectly fine with him as he was used to padding his shoes with old newspaper to make them fit. He smiled to himself. This turned out to be good because he had an idea of how to obtain soap from the camp without raising suspicion.

"I'll be back tomorrow," he said.

"I know you will," answered the priest.

"Be careful," Karl said, "You know too much."

"I know that we need each other. Let's try and build on that," the old man answered.

The next morning during the early drill which required that all the boys line up in rows of three and doing knee bends for 5 minutes and running in place for 10 minutes, Karl went through the personal belongings of his charges and collected all of the started soap bars he could find. He wound up with a bag of over 120 of partially used-up bars of soap of all sizes. He figured that it weight more than three pounds. Then he went to the camp supply room and took from the soap supply a fresh box and removed about 140 new bars and issued the new bars to the kids as they reentered the building.

"I had to confiscate all the old soap," he told camp commander Hardfeld, who stared at him in amazement as Karl handed him a new bar, "where is yours?"

Hardfeld went to his room and came back with 2 started bars.

"What's wrong with the soap we are using?"

"Beats me," Karl answered and mumbled under his breath something about a sabotage report from Berlin. Lieutenant Hardfeld just nodded, sabotage was on everyone's mind and coming from Berlin was frightening.

Actually, as of late, anything coming from Berlin or connected to Berlin was bad news. He just wished that the whole darn war would be over. He wanted to go home to Hannover and see if his family was still alive. Besides constant reports of bombing attacks by allied forces on Hannover, he had not heard a word from his family in weeks. It was starting to wear. Just as little as two months ago he was in weekly contact through the use of Feldpost, a term for military mail. But since then everything changed for the worse. Feldpost was not able to keep up with the constantly changing of positions and commands. He was more than discouraged; he knew he was a cripple for the rest of his life, however short that might be. The KLV camp meant nothing to him and he just wanted to see his family once more.

He nodded to Karl, "Yes, do what you can to keep us healthy and in compliance with Berlin's latest nonsense."

He knew that his last words were dangerous, because any criticism of Berlin in any form or way was strictly forbidden. He regretted his remark and was ready to back-paddle, but luckily Karl did not seem to notice. He was already on the way to the dump to get rid of a pair of dirty paper bags, or something.

Good thing that Karl and Peter are efficient, he thought to himself, I would not really know how to keep order in this place or keep the children occupied and healthy.

But, still he wondered about Karl and his connections to Berlin.

Lothar Hardfeld knew that Karl's connections must be powerful because every so often, Karl was ordered to Berlin for a one day meeting with HJ leaders and political officials. One of the latest achievements of Karl was a total and unexpected surprise for Hardfeld.

Karl was called to Berlin for a three-day stay and when he returned he did so on a motorcycle with a sidecar filled with cans of petrol.

"Where did you get this and what for," he had asked, and Karl had looked at him.

"This is for you," he said, "my orders are to get you and the boys back to Berlin in case the Russians break our lines by Warschau, and I am told that transportation at that time will be very limited, but I am supposed to act to the best of my ability in accordance with my orders. Do you like it?"

"What?" Lothar asked, "Your orders, which seem to override my authority, or the bike?"

"The bike of course, my older friend. You are unable to march for any distance and my orders are directly from the SS headquarters and in writing."

With this he started to hand Lothar two SS insignia envelopes, but before Karl let go of them, he kept one of the envelopes and put it back in the his pocket.

"I like the bike already," Hardfeld answered as he briefly glanced at the envelope, "but how did you get it? And where did you learn how to drive?"

"Wehrmacht and a crash course of the HJ," was the short answer.

"But where did you get it, and the petrol?"

Karl looked over the shoulder of Lothar and seemed to observe a bird in the distance. There was a moment of silence and then, "Don't ask."

"How are you supposed to bring the boys to Berlin if there is no transportation?"

Again, there was a moment of silence. Karl was by now concentrating hard on the bird. "My problem," he answered, "I will ask for your help when I need it." With this he turned away and pushed the motorcycle to an empty storage shed on the opposite side of the cloister.

It had been snowing for a while and the envelope in Lothar's hand was getting wet. It contained two sheets of paper informing him and ordering him that in the event of a breakthrough of Russian forces, the camp was to be evacuated to Berlin under the command of Karl Veth, Gefolgschaftsfuehrer, HJ. Furthermore, he was relieved of his command due to his physical inability to act in the face of the enemy.

The second sheet of paper was just an information sheet advising him that due to the need of keeping fighting troops and reserve units supplied with food and weapons, an evacuation of his camp by rails was highly unlikely.

It closed with the sentence, 'We wish you and Gefolgschaftsfuehrer Karl Veth all the best in your endeavor to bring the children home to their parents. Heil Hitler.'

It was signed Berlin School Evacuation Headquarters.

Dated February 6th 1945.

The Lieutenant could not help staring at the papers in his hand. All his efforts to be an example as an officer and all his sacrifices had been in vain.

He considered himself to be an officer of the Wehrmacht, and not subject to the command of the SS or the HJ. To be replaced by a 14-year-old kid in the uniform of the HJ was just too much for him to comprehend.

He considered for a moment to end it all, but the thought of his family and of the motorcycle in the shed made him hesitate just long enough to abandon his thought of taking his own life. There had to be a way out. How, he did not know, and neither did he know how to ride a motorcycle. Maybe the answer was with Karl. After all, if the SS and the HJ put him in command, then maybe the boy was also capable of getting him home. He took another pain killer pill and realized that he had only a few left.

TWO

When Karl was in Berlin, six weeks ago, he had thought of a possible way to get the children back to Berlin.

Actually it was not so much his plan, than a variation of a plan which was given to him in the first week of February during a meeting with a few of the remaining school officials in Berlin.

The instructions outlining the plan were titled "Extreme Evacuation Guidelines" and he had been told to "modify" as necessary. Karl had modified this plan immediately.

While still in Berlin, he went to the local HJ headquarters seeking additional authorization documents. Then he tried to find and see a certain SS commander who happened to be the father of one of the boys in his camp.

After about an hour of searching through the files of the school district, he found what he had looked for and decided to visit the local SS headquarters. The SS commander he wanted to see however was unavailable. So he left a note for SS Obersturmbannfuehrer von Glinski, informing him that his son Udo was one of his charges, but he could not assure the Obersturmbannfuehrer the safe return of his son in case of a Russian breakthrough. He ended the note, "I would appreciate any pertinent help." He signed the letter and hoped it would reach the SS commander.

Karl had also tried during this Berlin visit to find his own parents, which he had not seen since the previous May, but the apartment house where they had lived for the last 4 years was totally destroyed during an air attack in early January by allied forces. All that was left was rubble of broken cement pieces. On some of the larger pieces were scribbled messages from former tenants, in an effort to leave a message for relatives or friends who were seeking to find the whereabouts of survivors.

Karl found nothing, but he was not too worried. In one of the last letters from his mother, she had told him that she and his younger brother and sister were trying to leave Berlin and she had named an address of an uncle in Westphalia. Still, he was seeking to find a notice from his father who was drafted into the Volkssturm, but as much as he looked within the short time period he had available, he found nothing. No note, no address, and no indication from any neighbor he used to know.

He did find however, a larger piece of rubble with a list of people who did not survive the bombing of this house, and his family was not listed.

He considered this to be good news. Actually, much better than he had feared. He had scribbled with a sharp piece of broken metal on one of the cement pieces, his name and the current date. This way, he figured, if someone from his family was looking for him, they would know that on this date he was still alive.

Karl then hurried to meet the military transport column which took supplies to the fighting front in Poland and who was ordered to take him along as far as Kosten; about 10 kilometers from the children's camp. He was running late and he almost missed the convoy, which was just leaving as he turned the last corner leading to the supply depot.

While he was frantically waiving to the first drivers it was not until after the fourth truck had passed that he was able to jump on the running board of the fifth truck and show his credentials. The driver was an old gray haired reserve soldier, and he slowed down just enough for Karl to jump on the running board and climb into the back of the truck.

In a way he was lucky, because the first few trucks all had open truck beds while the one he was able to catch had a canvas top and seemed to carry medical supplies. It had started to snow and Karl crawled over boxes and crates to find some shelter from the cold wind which blew in from the rear through the holes in the canopy. He was exhausted and fell asleep as soon as he found a place protected from the howling wind. When he woke up it was almost daylight. The convoy had come to a halt and the drivers were busy clearing a massive and almost frozen snowdrift from an intersection.

Karl crawled to the loading gate at the rear of the truck and asked the next driver who walked by how much longer it would take to reach his drop off point by Kosten. The soldier just stared at Karl's HJ uniform and answered that he did not know the exact time frame, but it would take at least another hour. This was perfectly alright with Karl. He was afraid that the convoy had stopped for him to get off and that he might have to start his walk to the camp. He searched his pocket for some dried bread, which he had received from the school officials the previous day.

He did not really know how hungry he was until he started to chew on the bread. It was called Knaeckebrot and in a texture similar to rye crispy. Not bad tasting, but a bit salty. He ate every last crumb he had and then jumped out of the truck to help the drivers moving the snow away from the intersection to what appeared to be a major highway.

Thirty minutes later he was back in the truck.

After another hour and a half, he was awakened by his driver, who pointed out to him the general direction he had to walk to reach his camp.

The snowstorm was gone. However, the country road he was supposed to follow was buried under a foot of fresh snow. It made for some difficult walking, but after a little while the sun was penetrating the gray sky and the landscape turned from flat white to a sometimes blinding white with some glaring blue spots; it almost looked pretty.

It was the typical Polish flat plain with just enough of some straggly birch trees from time to time to mark the direction of the road. Karl was feeling great. The soldiers had given him some more Knaeckebrot, and a small can of margarine as well as a can of meat. He had also been given a field canteen of water, which he had not even started to open when he finally reached the camp.

During his walk he had tried to imagine what he needed to do if the Russians broke through the defense line in eastern Poland. He knew that the 'Evacuation Guidelines" given to him in Berlin were almost impossible to implement. He had been given some authorization documents which empowered him to stop any kind of empty vehicles, including military vehicles which he might encounter as he marched the children westward to Berlin. As a next step, he was supposed to hand the drivers of the vehicles the orders to take the children to safety.

Right on the outset, two things were almost impossible to achieve. For one thing, the children of the camp were all between the ages of 10 years and 12 years old, and marching in a snowstorm would be a suicide mission.

Besides that, what about the food and water?

The second part of stopping military vehicles might work, if there is an orderly retreat, and Karl was not too sure about that. Besides, he had not even seen any empty military vehicles. The few trucks he had seen moving westward were filled with wounded soldiers, and the ones moving eastward were filled with supplies and reserve troops.

His thoughts turned constantly back to his evolving friendship and arrangement with the Polish priest. He had started to like the old fellow and he had learned that his name was Stanislaus Dobrowski.

During the last week, Karl had kungled with him for additional used civilian clothing and now had pants and jackets for Peter and Hardfeld as well as for himself.

He had also asked Stanislaus if he could introduce him to some Polish guides. He needed some local knowledge to find a short cut through a birch forest to the railroad track, which connected Warsaw with Kottbus. This was two weeks ago, and in the meantime, he had supplied Stanislaus with some more canned food and some medical supplies.

His general idea was to obligate the priest to help him and the boys when the time came to evacuate the camp.

And the time was now.

The Russians had broken the German lines. There was not much the few retreating German tank and infantry units could do to stop the Russian onslaught towards Berlin.

Karl had entered the passageway to the chapel, and looked for his stash of clothes. He found everything just as he had left it and he kept on running towards the end of the underground passageway. He was trying to locate Stanislaus and hoped that the old fellow would really keep his word and help him. He did not need to worry. The priest had gotten the word of the massive German retreat through his resistance network before Karl had even heard it on the radio.

"Over here," he shouted at Karl, who just turned around the corner towards the altar.

Karl turned and was stunned for a moment. Next to Stanislaus were three young men, obviously Poles, maybe 17 or 18 years of age. At first he thought he was being ambushed and considered reaching for his service pistol, which he carried under his shirt. But then his worry turned into surprise because he saw several large baskets of apples standing between the three of them. Karl had not eaten an apple for over a year and he could not even remember when he saw the last one.

"The Russians are coming," was all he was able to say as he still stared at the green and yellow apples.

"We know," answered Stanislaus, "but, according to our information, it is only a tank division. Their infantry is still standing down and will not move for a few hours."

"It does not matter, tanks or infantry," answered Karl, "the children have to leave immediately." At this time they all could hear the howling sound of the camp siren. Peter or Hardfeld must have triggered the alarm.

"Yes," said Stanislaus, "this is why you see my friends here. They will help you to get the boys to the railroad tracks. They will also help you to light a fire to stop the train." When he saw Karl's skeptical look, the priest continued, "You will need them."

"What for?" asked Karl, "You know yourself how difficult it will be to explain their presence to an SS patrol or commando. If they will be seen with the German children they will be shot regardless of what I say."

"I already thought of that." answered Stanislaus, "These fellows speak a good enough German to pass as Volksdeutsche."

Volksdeutsche was the term used for non-native Germans. They were actually Poles as far as their legal status was concerned, but they were of German ancestry.

Karl looked at the group in bewilderment. He could not believe what he was hearing.

"You cannot take the risk," he insisted, "you are lucky that you are alive as it is, and I don't understand what is in it for you?"

The priest answered by handing Karl an apple, "Don't worry, they have German papers, and if one of your little boys falls or passes out in the cold, you will be unable to carry him and you would have to leave him behind; so you will need these guys, and," he locked eyes with Karl, "don't ask me about my motivation again. It hurts."

Karl nodded, "I understand, sorry."

Karl turned towards the largest of the three, "What is your name?"

"I am Elu, this is my brother Lechek and we call the other guy Pilu. Here are my German papers." With this Elu handed Karl a German Volksdeutschen Ausweis, which was the identification card issued by the German civilian authorities.

"This one looks authentic to me." Karl said as he glanced at the seal and date of issue, "Let me see the other ones."

Lechek stepped forward and handed him two more ID's, which looked identical to the one which Elu had shown him.

"Well, let's hope you don't need them." Karl was satisfied with the quality of the Ausweise, he had seen worse. "What is with these apples?" he asked Stanislaus.

"They are for your children as a farewell present and as a thank you gift for helping us when we needed your support."

For a moment it looked to Karl as if the priest had some tears in his eyes.

But, time was pressing and he had more on his mind than to think about the sentimental attitude displayed by Stanislaus.

He turned to Elu, "Please place the baskets with the apples near the rear gate of the inner wall, and then watch for our group leaving in about an hour."

With that he turned to Stanislaus, "Watch out for yourself, you are facing a much worse enemy than we Germans ever were to you. If the Russians find out that you cooperated with us, you will be a dead man. Besides that, get rid of your clergy clothes. The first wave of fighting troops will be happy to have any excuse to shoot you."

The old priest all of the sudden did not seem so old anymore. He stood erect as he nodded to Karl. "I know that our days may be numbered, and even if the fighting troops spare us, the political commissioners might not."

"I wish you well," said Karl, "and thank you once more for all your help.

"I will not forget you old man, and I know that you are not a priest."

With that he turned around, waved once more to Stanislaus and disappeared into the passageway.

He heard Stanislaus asking a question but he could not afford to waste any more time to stop and answer. He had to get back to Hardfeld and inform him of his idea of stopping a train to get the boys back to Berlin.

As he returned to the main hallway, he almost ran in to his friend Peter.

"Where have you been? I think Hardfeld had a stroke or heart attack. He is lying on the floor in the kitchen." He grabbed Karl by the arm and pulled him across the assembly hall to the part of the cloister, which served as a kitchen.

Karl took a careful look at Hardfeld and decided that Hardfeld had neither experienced a heart attack nor a stroke. The skid marks on the floor indicated that he must have slipped on the greasy floor and then passed out. One of the two Polish women who served as a camp cook was kneeling by the Lieutenant and trying to push a towel under his head.

"Get me a pot of water!" Karl shouted at Peter. "No, cold water, quick!" he added as he saw Peter scanning the stove for a pot.

While Peter was searching for a suitable pot, Karl rose up and grabbed a bucket of water that stood next to the doorway. With one fast swoop, he threw the contents of the bucket over Hardfeld's head and shook him by the shoulders. "Wake up!" Karl shouted, "Wake up, wake up!"

As Hardfeld slowly opened his eyes, Peter approached from behind and dumped another load of cold water over the Lieutenant's head. It took another effort by Karl shouting questions at Hardfeld until the Lieutenant was able to answer.

"No, I don't think that I hit my head. I must have passed out from the pain when I fell on my amputated arm stump." Hardfeld sat up and noticed that he was sitting in a pool of dirty water. "Who did this to me?" Peter and Karl helped him up and pushed a wooden bench under his buckling knees. "And, what is going on?" Apparently he was clueless and pretty useless in the current situation.

"I'll bring you up to date in a moment," Karl answered, "but right now I have to know where you keep the Camp Evacuation Registration Box."

"In my office, should be on the top shelf, first box on the right."

"Good, and where is your pain medication?"

"Should be right here in my pocket." With this the Lieutenant reached into his pants pockets, apparently searching for his vial of pills.

"Run to the office and get the box with the registration forms." Karl shoved Peter in the direction of the door. He then turned to Hardfeld; "The Russians broke the defense line about 180 kilometer east from here. I will walk the boys through the woods to the railroad tracks and try to stop a train going west. I will then come back and get you out of here."

Hardfeld just stared at him in utter disbelief. "You cannot do that. It will be impossible to achieve. I have to command you to stay here with me!"

"You can command all you want, this is your privilege, but as you very well know, I don't have to obey. You can either try to walk with us, or you can stay here until I return. Your choice, Lieutenant!"

While Hardfeld pondered a reply, Karl went into the assembly hall where all the boys were seated at their designated dining tables. This is the easy part, Karl thought to himself. The camp had practiced for the last two weeks all kinds of emergency procedures, and this one here was indeed the easiest to implement and hopefully to execute.

As he entered the hall he overheard one of the boys whispering to his classmate, "This is no exercise tonight, Rudy, look at Karl, he is all serious. Not his regular manner and not a smile on his lips."

Karl turned to the boy, "You like to see me smile?" and then louder so that all the boys could hear him, "Listen up, this is not a drill, none of us will go back to bed, and all of us will be going home."

He had hoped for a happy response, but it was not as joyful as he had expected.

Most of the boys seemed happy over the news, but there were also boys crying in bewilderment, and more than a few were just staring at the floor. He knew right away what was wrong.

The mail had been slow over the last two weeks and some of the boys had not gotten a letter from home in over three weeks. These boys feared that they would not find their mothers alive. Some feared that their apartments had been 'bombed out' and in this case 'going home' was not possible. Where would they wind up, when there was not a 'home' to go to? Where would they go in Berlin when the little security of this camp and Hardfeld and Karl was no longer available?

Karl knew he had to inject some glimmer of hope otherwise some of the boys might just give up when they needed all their strength to endure the walk to the railroad.

"Listen up again!" he yelled through the tumult, "I know that some of you have been waiting from a letter from home, but there is really nothing to worry about. As you know, I was in Berlin just a few days ago and was told that the mail to the camps had been delayed in favor of the field post to our wounded soldiers.

I can also tell you that there was no major air attack on Charlottenburg during the last two weeks. Most of the air attacks had been targeted at Tempelhof and Neukoelln."

His words had the desired impact because the boys in his camp had all been from the school district of Charlottenburg and

Wilmersdorf.

"In one hour from now I will lead you through the woods to the railroad line to Berlin. Once we are there we will board a train and when we reach Berlin, we will proceed to the Fichte school in Wilmersdorf where you will be met by your relatives. Your relatives have been advised that you will be there within 48 hours."

Karl was lying to the best of his abilities. He knew that he could not provide any real answers, but he also knew that he had to keep the boys motivated enough to sustain the upcoming walk through the snow and the remainder of the night.

"Peter will call out your names and hand you your identification card. The card will be in an envelope attached to a string, which you will loop around your neck. All of you will stay in this hall. Eat as much as you wish in the meantime.

We will be on our way within 15 minutes."

As Peter proceeded to call out the names and hand out the ID envelopes, Karl noticed that someone was calling his name. The shouting came from the outside of the buildings, but there was no one supposed to be outside except for Elu, Lechek and Pilu, the three Polish guides he had met a while ago.

He looked at Hardfeld, who had followed him into the assembly hall.

"Did you hear that," he asked.

"Hear what," answered the Lieutenant, who could hardly keep himself upright.

A dreadful thought entered Karl's mind. Hardfeld is in worse shape than I thought, first a cripple and now also deaf.

"Jungscharfuehrer Karl Veth, is anybody in there?"

Karl heard it again and went outside into the cold wind and looked around.

The sky was clear and the moon was out and he could recognize a soldier at the gate to the camp's training ground.

"Coming!" he yelled on the top of his lungs and then he also saw what looked like a military truck outside the gate.

The gate was closed, but not locked. As he neared the gate, the soldier stopped shouting and waited for him to come closer. Karl looked over the soldier for a second and knew that he had an SS man in front of him. No rank insignia was visible, but Karl liked him instantly without knowing why.

Maybe because he saw two small military transport trucks lined up in front of the gate.

The SS man looked at Karl for a moment, "I need to speak with Karl Veth."

"That would be me," answered Karl.

"Cannot be," the SS soldier replied, "you are just a dumb kid from the camp."

Karl pointed to the insignia on his uniform and to the silver eagle on his cap.

"Believe it or not, I am Karl, and I am happy to see your trucks. I am authorized to command any empty military trucks to assist me in the evacuation of this camp. Here are my papers."

The soldier, who looked like he was about 50 years old, squinted first at the papers and then at Karl's insignia on the uniform and when he saw the silver eagle on the black winter cap of the Hitler Youth uniform, his mouth moved without saying a word.

He finally managed a few words, "My name is Brandt. I am coming here at the direct orders of SS Obersturmbannfuehrer von Glinski. I am supposed to bring his son Udo back to Berlin, and in doing so to render any assistance required by Jungscharfuehrer Karl Veth. I guess this is you, but I was under the impression that Veth was older then you are, and that Veth is trained as a sniper."

Karl just looked at Brandt and asked, "How many children are you able to transport in your trucks, and how much petrol do you have on board?"

Brandt still had trouble associating Karl Veth with the kid in front of him.

The uniform and the papers convinced him that Karl was the Hitler Youth he was looking for, and Obersturmbannfuehrer von Glinski had warned him not to underestimate Karl Veth in any way, but this boy looked so small and seemingly much too young to represent any authority at all.

"I can transport between 60 and 70 kids at the most and I have sufficient fuel to get back to Berlin," he answered to Karl's question.

"Sixty to 70 will not do; not even close Herr Brandt, but we will see. Come in and if you are hungry we have food to share. Please back up your trucks to the side entrance over there." Karl pointed to one of the several doors leading to inside the building and opened the gate.

THREE

Brandt went back to his truck and motioned to the driver of the second truck to follow him into the yard. As Brandt backed up his truck to the old wooden door of the cloister, he scanned the dark sky for clouds. There were none. The snowstorm had passed a few hours ago and he could see stars wherever he looked. He went over to his younger buddy in the other truck and told him about this Hitler Youth kid who was in charge of the boy's camp.

"You will not believe this fellow, Anton, but as you know, our orders are to assist him and to follow his instructions. But as of right now we are invited to go in and eat."

"How did he know that we are starving?" wondered Anton. "By the way, did you see the three fellows on the far side of the yard? It looked to me as if they were trying to hide from us and now I don't see them anymore."

"No," answered Brandt, "I was only looking at this kid in the uniform of an HJ leader. And I am still worried about our mission here.

"Sturmbannfuehrer von Glinski told us that we would find more boys here than we could accommodate. We might be triggering a panic when we leave some of them behind. I am glad that we are not in command or the decision maker."

He flicked his just started cigarette in a nearby snow bank. "Let's go in, and remind me to tell Karl about the three unknowns you saw."

Karl was standing in the hallway, next to Hardfeld and Peter.

"Everything changed," Karl announced, "we have a partial solution to our dilemma. The father of Udo von Glinski, the SS leader of our district in Berlin, must have gotten my message that I cannot vouch for the safe return of his son to Berlin. We have some trucks waiting to take more than half of the boys back to Berlin."

"Trucks," echoed Hardfeld "where? And Udo? I had no special

information about his parents, how did you know?" He really did not expect an answer to his question as Karl was always preoccupied and lately thinking ahead of him. But this time, to his surprise, Karl answered.

"When I received the order to bring the children back to Berlin, I reviewed the current school records to see if any of their parents had been killed during the air attacks and I came upon Udo von Glinski's father, listed as Sturmbannfuehrer of the 'Waffen SS'. I tried to find him and tried to call him to enlist his help in case we had to evacuate the camp. However, all I could do was to leave a message for him at the SS Headquarters."

Before Karl could finish his answer, Peter had sneaked a look outside the front door and then left for the assembly hall.

"Udo," he called, "Udo von Glinski, come to the front table." The boys in the hall repeated Peter's call until a blonde boy showed up at the front table. Peter knew him well. Udo was 11 years old and one of his best long distance runners and he also liked him because of his always-disciplined behavior.

"Udo," he asked him, "is your father an SS leader?"

"I am not supposed to talk about my parents." answered Udo, "Did something happened to my father?"

"No," Peter assured him, "Your father is all right. Now just get your belongings and bring your friends and sit down here at this table."

While Hardfeld limped through the outside door and looked at the two small trucks, Karl saw the two SS men who just came out of the kitchen, each with a dish full of steaming mashed potatoes and gravy.

"Sit down," he said, "how long will it take you to drive to Berlin?"

"Depending upon congestion around the towns, troop movements, delays and weather, we should make it within eight hours," answered Brandt.

"Do you have enough fuel to make a detour of less than two hours," asked Karl.

"Yes, we do." This was the first time that Anton answered. "But, I don't think that a detour is called for. We drove a pretty direct route to get here and I have been driving this route now several times, transporting wounded troops, and I know my way around the area."

"I am glad that you know your way," answered Karl. "The detour is not exactly a detour, but a side trip. We cannot fit all the boys in your trucks, and we cannot leave any behind. So I need you to drive some of them to the railroad line leading west, probably to Kottbus. You will then return to pick up the remaining group and take them to Berlin. I will be with you on the side trip, and then you will be on your own."

Brandt looked at Anton. "This sounds better than leaving screaming kids behind. Let's do this as fast as possible." He then turned to Karl, "You might not be as isolated as you think you are. Upon our arrival we saw three guys without uniforms, probably Polish resistance, trying to hide and stay out of view."

"Yes, they are, and they are also known to me. I will get them right now." Karl got up and left the surprised SS men to the remainder of their meal.

Peter, who had just approached the table, followed Karl. "You know Polish resistance members? I don't know any more if I really know you; I mean how can I trust you?"

Karl smiled at his friend. "Come along. I'll even give you an apple and introduce you."

Hardfeld, still standing at the door, overheard Peter's question and Karl's answer.

"Karl, I demand an honest answer to Peter's questions."

Karl stopped in his stride. "Yes, I understand that you are both confused, but we have not sufficient time for long explanations. So I'll make it short. By coincidence I met some Polish resistance members, solicited their help for the sake of the boys, traded some food to obtain some civilian clothes for you Hardfeld, and for you Peter, and if you don't trust me you might as well start walking to Berlin right now. You can also choose to help me to get the boys organized."

"Civilian clothes," mumbled Hardfeld, "Truck's, one miracle after another. What do you want me to do?"

"Yeah," Peter chimed in, "what do you need us to do?"

Karl looked at both of them. "Hardfeld, line up 40 boys and try to get them all inside of one truck. This will be a very close fit. See how many you can fit into one truck. Two or three might sit next to the driver. Once you know the number for both of the trucks select the youngest and weakest ones for the later ride to Berlin.

"Peter, select about 40 of the oldest and strongest boys and have them collect their bedding straw and blankets and pile them up at the exit where the trucks are standing. I'll be right back."

Karl broke into a short run towards the other side of the yard and Hardfeld and Peter returned to the main building. Elu came out of the bushes he was hiding in and intercepted Karl in his run.

"I see the trucks, is our plan dismissed?"

"No, but we don't have to walk, we will drive. Get your friends and bring the apples to the front door and prepare to leave with us."

Karl lifted one of the baskets on his shoulder and started his walk back to the trucks. Elu and his friends carried the rest of the baskets close behind him. As they approached the vehicles they were greeted by the first group of boys who climbed all over the first truck and over themselves. Hardfeld tried to get some resemblance of order into the bunch by shouting short and sharp orders. It seemed to work for a moment and then he had to repeat them again.

Karl set his basket down and called to the group. "Line up in a single line.

"One apple for each of you, come and get them while you can."

The boys were almost stunned as if they could not believe their ears and eyes. They did not remember that apples existed.

To the amazement of the Lieutenant, they lined up in a single file. Karl ordered the first boy at the bushel to stand by and give each of the other boys one apple. Not of their choice of course, just one unselected apple to each one of the group. Karl waved at Elu and Lechek and helped Pilu to bring their baskets into the hall.

It took only a few minutes and all of the apples disappeared from sight.

Every one of the boys had indeed received an apple of their own.

They stood around munching the juicy treat, and talking to each other, describing the taste of the yellow apple to the ones who had received a green apple and vice-versa.

Even Hardfeld had an apple and was debating with himself to ask Karl how he had managed this new miracle. But again, Karl was ahead of him.

"The apples are a present, I did nothing special. As a matter of fact, I am just as surprised as you are. Now tell me how many boys fit into one truck?"

"Forty-two," answered Hardfeld, "this includes two boys next to the driver. What's next?"

"Easy," said Karl, "just like I told you before. Line up eighty-four of the youngest or weakest boys and keep them busy carrying food from the kitchen to the door here. Also tell them to dress as warm as they can and no suitcases. Backpacks only, with a bare minimum of belongings.

"I will take the rest to the railroad and come back with the empty trucks."

"You mean to say that you will leave the boys alone at the railroad bed? What are they supposed to do? How will they survive," asked Hardfeld.

"You will see," answered Karl, "because you will be with me." He looked across the hall and went to see Peter.

"Hey, Peter, how are you coming along? Did you get all of the blankets?"

"Of course, no big thing, and I also figured the numbers between the railroad group and the truck group and I have the oldest boys standing by," answered Peter, "We are ready to roll at your word."

"Let's first get the canned food from the storage room to the trucks. Line up the boys and order fire brigade drill. Where are the drivers? They should help."

"Hmm," answered Peter, "I think Anton likes our kitchen helper, Regina. They made eyes at each other and disappeared a moment ago from the kitchen. Herr Brandt is outside by his truck."

Karl had absolutely no experience in handling a situation like Anton and Regina. He was old enough to shoot and to kill if necessary. He had been trained by extremely good teachers, but nobody had ever told him anything of sex or even a subject close to it.

However, he did know that the Russian soldiers mostly attacked when they were drunk and he had been told that when the fighting troops are drunk they would rape any women and girls they come across, even very young girls who are still children. But, this here had nothing to do with fighting troops or raping.

He went outside to see Brandt and told him about the disappearance of Anton and Regina. "I don't know how to handle this and we have to get on the way as soon as possible. Please help me," he asked of Brandt.

"I don't really know Anton that well," answered Brandt, "but this should not take me long. Get the boys on board and I'll take care of him."

Brandt went into the building and Karl signaled to Peter to bring his group of older boys to the trucks.

"All of you will listen to me and to me only," he addressed the boys.

"You will sit wherever you find a place to sit. Peter and I will throw all the blankets and bedding on top of you. Sit on it and cover yourself. The ride will be short, not longer than 30 minutes at the most.

You, Willy, will sit in the front, next to the driver of truck number two. Peter and Pilu will sit with the rest of you in the back of truck number two.

"Lechek and I will sit with the group in the back of truck number one. Elu will be in the front of truck number one, next to the driver. That's all, no questions. Load the canned food and then get on the trucks!"

Within twenty minutes the boys climbed on their assigned trucks. Peter and Karl proceeded to pile all of the blankets and bedding on top of them. As Peter lifted the last of the bedding into the truck, he looked to his friend and asked, "How come you decided to sit in the back with the boys, instead of in the front next to Brandt?"

Karl glanced at him, "Elu knows the nearest way to the railroad bed. I have never been there and could not be of any help to the driver, and I don't think that you have been there either. Besides, I want to talk to Lechek."

Peter nodded in agreement but then asked, "What gives with Lechek?"

"I don't really know for sure, but I think that Lechek is the younger brother or even the son of Wanda, our camp cook. And, I have the feeling that our Polish crew is just as much afraid of the Russians as we are."

Karl went back into the building to look for Brandt and get the civilian clothes for Hardfeld and Peter. He decided that he would leave his own jacket and pants in his room until he came back from the trip to the railroad.

The clothes for Peter looked like the right size, maybe a little too small for Peter's large frame, but they had to do. As he came out of his room he saw Wanda, the older of the Polish cooks come out of the kitchen.

"Hello Wanda, have you seen Regina?"

"Yes," answered Wanda, "she is outside talking to the SS driver. I think she is trying to hitch a ride away from here."

Karl did not care if Regina wanted to get away from the Russians, but he did care if this would mean that one of his boys had to surrender his seat on the truck. Still carrying the bundle of clothes for Peter and Hardfeld, he turned to the outside door but stopped when he saw Wanda's face. It was all red and tears were running down her cheeks.

"Karl," she said, "can you take us along? Please? You are our last hope. If the Russians find out, and they will, that we worked in this camp for the Germans, there will be no mercy for us."

"Even if we could take you along, where would you go to in Berlin?" Karl answered, as he hurried towards the door. "And what about Stanislaus? You told me that he is your father and that he is part of the Polish resistance. I am sure that he can find a way to hide you."

The disappointment on Wanda's face and her frightened eyes made him stop to reconsider. His thoughts raced through his mind. Just a week ago, everybody, he included, was afraid of the Polish underground spies. And now it looked like that they wanted to be friends with the Germans. He thought for a moment about Stanislaus, who had assigned three of his young members to guide him and his boys through the woods to the railroad tracks. That was just about an hour ago.

Things were changing fast, much too fast for him to comprehend. He needed to talk with adults who had experience. Hardfeld and Brandt were the only adults around him, and he was not too sure about Hardfeld's mental condition.

Karl thought about his father and wondered if he would have had an answer for him. The last time he had seen him was about one year ago; and right now he did not even know if his father was still alive.

Wanda was still looking at him. "Please," she whispered.

"I don't know myself what I am doing, Wanda. This situation is not in my hands and I am afraid of making any decision at all. But, let's talk with your father. Tell him I need to see him when I come back from the railroad."

Hardfeld had seen Wanda and Karl at the door and he had also seen the civilian clothes Karl had been carrying.

"Are they all yours?" he asked Karl.

"No, they are yours and Peter's. Hide yours in the sidecar of the motorbike. As soon as I am back we will get the boys on the road and you and I will take the motorbike and join up with our group at the railroad."

Karl handed a heavy insulated overcoat, a jacket, and a pair of trousers to Hardfeld. "Oh, I almost forgot, I also got you a packet of high potency pain killers. You will find them in the pocket of the jacket."

Hardfeld was speechless. He had always asked the military field doctor, who came by the camp every second week, for additional pain killers and was told every time that he could only get one pill for each day because they were in very short supply and needed for the field hospitals. And now he was holding in his hand a vial full of pills. There must be at least 60 tablets here, he thought.

He trembled as he put the vial in his pants pocket. He had no idea how Karl could get his hand on medication while he himself as an officer was unable to do so.

Karl handed the remainder of the clothing to Peter and turned to Brandt.

"Ready to drive? Let's go."

Elu took his seat next to Brandt and Karl climbed in the back. He found a place next to Lechek.

While the trucks moved out, Hardfeld turned to the remaining boys, "You will be going home within the next two hours. It will be cold on the trucks. See if you can get into your shoes with two pairs of socks on, and double up on your clothing as much as you can wear. Also, you cannot take any suitcases along, only backpacks.

"Go to the storage room and fill your back packs with canned food. If you don't have a can opener on your pocketknife, go into the kitchen and see if Wanda or Regina can find you one. Furthermore, go through all the rooms and bring all the pillows and blankets that the first group might have left behind. You don't have much time, so let's get going."

Hardfeld thought hard if he had forgotten anything, hoping that it would not be anything critical. He then looked at Udo who was still sitting on the front table. "Get two or three of your friends and help me to push the motorbike into the yard."

The lieutenant felt a little relieved that this camp assignment was almost over, but he was also deeply worried about the upcoming challenge at the railroad, and how, or even if, he would eventually get home himself. He went to his room and stuffed his backpack with some underwear and socks and then carried his last personal belongings and notes to the kitchen where he burned them in the wood stove.

ABOUT THE AUTHOR

Horst Christian was born in Berlin, Germany in 1930. His father, a mathematician and a banker, taught him to read and write before the age of 5. He discovered his love for writing by the time he was 10 years old and wrote vacation reports and several articles for the German school periodical "Hilf Mit."

When Horst was 10, he entered the "Jungvolk," a subdivision of the Hitler Youth, which was mandatory in the Berlin school system. He then entered the Hitler Youth at the age of 14, also mandatory, and continued writing for the Hitler Youth periodicals "Der Pimpf" and "Die Deutsche Jugend Burg."

His favorite pastime was playing in the U-Bahn (subway) tunnels. While other children played soccer, Horst, with a few other likeminded children, explored Berlin by riding the subway trains.

Drafted to help defend Berlin against the Soviets at the age of 14 because of his unique knowledge of the subway system, he served as a guide for various SS demolition commandos.

In the early 1950s, Horst immigrated to the United States and became a US citizen after the mandatory 5-year waiting period. He loves to travel and has visited all 50 states in the US, most of Europe, Canada, Mexico, the Caribbean and some Central American countries. He now resides with his wife Jennifer in Idaho.

HorstChristian.com

Made in the USA
Monee, IL
28 December 2021

87433956R00121